W9-DIG-527

"J. J. Carney creatively weaves the prophetic biographies of contemporary Catholic women and men into the fascinating cultural and intriguing socio-political history of Uganda. The combination of depth and clarity delivers a riveting account of the influence of Catholic social teaching on leadership in the local and public life of Uganda and in the global context. *For God and My Country* serves up a rich fare of insights into the dynamics of contemporary public theology."

—AGBONKHIANMEGHE E. OROBATOR, SJ, President of the Jesuit
Conference of Africa and Madagascar

"A penetrating and highly informative look into the history, public theology, and socio-political influence of the Catholic Church in Uganda in the late twentieth and early twenty-first centuries. Carney's easy and narrative style means that a broad audience of readers, both scholars and lay, in Africa and elsewhere, will find the book easily accessible and enjoyable to read."
—Emmanuel Katongole, Professor of Theology and Peace Studies, University of Notre Dame

"The unsung Romeros and Mother Teresas of Uganda are here deservedly celebrated and brilliantly showcased. More widely, this politically astute and ecclesially challenging book shows why Catholic social tradition cannot be captured in theory, concepts, or principles. Its heart and soul are 'performance'—in the cultures and crises that adapt it, correct it, and make it live. This work is a landmark intervention in Catholic theology and politics, both faithful and highly original."

—LISA SOWLE CAHILL, J. Donald Monan, SJ, Professor of Theology,
Boston College

"Thoughtfully prepared for a university classroom, *For God and My Country* uses well-chosen exemplary life-stories to explore the Ugandan Catholic presence since independence. Jay Carney skillfully blends historical scholarship, theological and ethical perspectives shaped by Catholic social teaching, and compelling narratives to produce portraits of leaders whose diverse heroism creates an inspiring legacy for Uganda's Catholic Church. The result is a unique work that brings contemporary global Catholic experience alive."

—PAUL KOLLMAN, CSC, Associate Professor of Theology,
University of Notre Dame

"Analyzing socio-political history through biographical embodiment of the claim for social justice and respect for human dignity is the innovative articulation of this book. J. J. Carney demonstrates that history is human and human is history, and that social change is often realized by the sacrifice of a few heroic individuals who are willing to lay down their lives for the rest of humanity, just like Jesus did. The author thus immortalizes the lives of Benedicto K. M. Kiwanuka, Emmanuel Cardinal Nsubuga, Fr. John Mary, Sr. Rose Mystica Muyinza, Tonino Pasolini, Sherry Meyer, and Rosalba Ato Oywa. These are heroes of evangelization in Uganda and Africa and their lives carry the legacy. This book would be relevant to readers in theology, African church and history, as well as social justice and political change."

—ELIAS OPONGO, SJ, Director of the Centre for Research, Training, and Publications (CRTP), Hekima University College, Nairobi, Kenya

"J. J. Carney's splendid *For God and My Country* tells the stories of seven Catholic leaders who embody the Church's prophetic social mission in postcolonial Uganda. Drawing on oral histories, Carney shows how their living faith 'fulfilled the gospel, today' (Luke 4:21) in their courageous pursuit of justice and reconciliation. In a world riven by violence and division, the lesson of these remarkable lives is both timely and truly 'catholic,' or universal."

—WILLIAM O'NEILL, SJ, Professor Emeritus, Jesuit School of Theology of Santa Clara University, and currently serving with the Jesuit Refugee Service in Nairobi, Kenya

For God and My Country

✝

STUDIES IN WORLD CATHOLICISM

Karen Kraft, *Managing Editor*

Other Titles in This Series

Beyond the Borders of Baptism: Catholicity, Allegiances, and Lived Identities. Edited by Michael L. Budde. Vol. 1, 2016. ISBN 9781498204736

New World Pope: Pope Francis and the Future of the Church. Edited by Michael L. Budde. Vol. 2, 2017. ISBN 9781498283717

Scattered and Gathered: Catholics in Diaspora. Edited by Michael L. Budde. Vol. 3, 2017. ISBN 9781532607097.

A Living Tradition: Catholic Social Doctrine and Holy See Diplomacy. A. Alexander Stummvoll. Vol. 4, 2018. ISBN 9781532605116.

Fragile World: Ecology and the Church. Edited by William T. Cavanaugh. Vol. 5, 2018. ISBN 9781498283403.

Love, Joy, and Sex: African Conversation on Pope Francis's Amoris Laetitia and the Gospel of Family in a Divided World. Edited by Stan Chu Ilo. Vol. 7, 2017. ISBN 9781532618956.

The Church and Indigenous Peoples in the Americas: In Between Reconciliation and Decolonization. Edited by Michel Andraos. Vol. 7, 2019. ISBN 9781532631115.

Pentecostalism, Catholicism, and the Spirit in the World. Edited by Stan Chu Ilo. Vol. 8, 2019. ISBN 9781532650352.

Gathered in my Name: Ecumenism in the World Church. Edited by William T. Cavanaugh. Vol. 9, 2020. ISBN 9781532685583.

Forthcoming Titles in This Series

A Church with the Indigenous Peoples: In Between Reconciliation and Decolonization. Michel Elias Andraos.

For God and My Country

Catholic Leadership in Modern Uganda

J. J. Carney

CASCADE *Books* · Eugene, Oregon

FOR GOD AND MY COUNTRY
Catholic Leadership in Modern Uganda

Studies in World Catholicism 10

Copyright © 2020 J. J. Carney. All rights reserved. Except for brief quotations in critical publications or reviews, no part of this book may be reproduced in any manner without prior written permission from the publisher. Write: Permissions, Wipf and Stock Publishers, 199 W. 8th Ave., Suite 3, Eugene, OR 97401.

Cascade Books
An Imprint of Wipf and Stock Publishers
199 W. 8th Ave., Suite 3
Eugene, OR 97401

www.wipfandstock.com

PAPERBACK ISBN: 978-1-5326-8252-0
HARDCOVER ISBN: 978-1-5326-8253-7
EBOOK ISBN: 978-1-5326-8254-4

Cataloguing-in-Publication data:

Names: Carney, J. J., author.

Title: For God and my country : Catholic leadership in modern Uganda / J. J. Carney.

Description: Eugene, OR : Cascade Books, 2020 | Series: Studies in World Catholicism 10 | Includes bibliographical references and index.

Identifiers: ISBN 978-1-5326-8252-0 (paperback) | ISBN 978-1-5326-8253-7 (hardcover) | ISBN 978-1-5326-8254-4 (ebook)

Subjects: LCSH: Catholic Church—Uganda—History. | Christian leadership—Catholic Church. | Catholic Church—Doctrines.

Classification: BX1682.U33 C37 2020 (print) | BX1682.U33 C37 (ebook)

Manufactured in the U.S.A.   OCTOBER 22, 2020

Figure01, Figure02, and Figure03: Uganda Political Map, Uganda's Catholic Dioceses, and Uganda's Precolonial Kingdoms, all written by Miles Irving

Figure04: Benedict K.M. Kiwanuka meets with President John F. Kennedy, 17 October 1961 (Abbie Rowe, White House Photographs, public domain photo used courtesy of John F. Kennedy Presidential Library and Museum, AR6843-B).

Figure05: Emmanuel Cardinal Nsubuga, private photo used by permission of Fr. Henry N. Kiwanuka

Figure06: Fr. John Mary Waliggo, private photo used by permission of Fr. Benedict Ssettuuma, Jr.

Figure07: Sr. Rose Mystica Muyinza, private photo used by permission of Sr. Theresa Basemera

To Fr. David Paul Baltz, MCCJ, and Fr. Joseph Kakooza Nyanzi:

For first showing me the transformative impact
of Catholic leadership in Uganda.

Contents

Illustrations

Acknowledgments

"THE MOST IMPORTANT INFORMATION is not in the archives—it is in our heads!" So Fr. Benedict Ssettuuma Jr. told me when I first began research on this book in 2015. Fr. Ssettuuma's counsel not only shaped the oral methodology that informs much of this book; it also captures my utter dependence on Ugandans for undertaking the audacious task of writing a book on the Catholic leaders who have shaped their country's religious and political history.

First and foremost, I thank my two primary Ugandan research assistants, Mr. George Mpanga and Mr. Herbert Busiku. Both are consummate professionals and tremendous people. George's research networks deeply informed my chapter on Sr. Rose Muyinza, and I am also grateful for his translation assistance on several of Cardinal Emmanuel Nsubuga's Luganda writings. Herbert introduced me to Rosalba Oywa and facilitated all of my interviews in the Gulu area. I also extend my heartfelt gratitude to Fr. Alex Kimpi who, during his seminarian years, assisted me with translations and initial research on the chapters concerning Sr. Rose Muyinza and Cardinal Nsubuga.

As attested in the bibliography and footnotes, much of this book's insight is drawn from oral interviews. I extend a special word of thanks to the living subjects of this book—Rosalba Oywa, Sherry Meyer, and Tonino Pasolini—for conducting multiple, lengthy interviews with me. In turn, I would like to acknowledge and thank the dozens of other Ugandans who sat with me for formal interviews concerning the subjects in this book: Justine Babirye, Sr. Theresa Basemera, Rachel Mirembe, Annette Nalugo, Specioza Namaggi, Leo Kibirango, Sr. Mary Cleophas at Nkonkojeru, Sr. Alma of the Little Sisters of St. Francis, Frankline Mbamanya Nsubuga, Teopista Lubega, Jones Mugume Amooti, Natal Gloria Birungi, Joseph Ddembe, Stella Bagwa, Tadeo Tebesigwa, Bridget Nanyunja, Jude Ssentle, Grace

Kahooza, Fr. Charles Kasibante, Josephine Tegamanyi, John Bosco Kabuye, Fred Matovu, Fred Mayanja, John Chrysostom Muyingo, Bishop Paul Sse-mogerere, Quilinous Otim, Franco Ojur, Pelegrine Otonga, Consi Ogwal, Mary Azore, Fred Middy Oluka-Oree, Fr. Cyprian Ocen P'acek, John Bosco Komakech Aludi, Chris Dolan, Steven Balmoi, Rwot Latim Baptist, Geof-frey Odong, Sheikh Musa Khelil, Mr. Okot Yasinto, Peter Wasswa Mpigi, Fr. Herman Kittuma, Msgr. George Serwanga, Msgr. Joseph Kasule, Fr. Denis Mayanja, Margaret Sekaggya, the late Med S.K. Kaggwa, John Ka-mya, Nathan Byamukama, Elizabeth Bosa, Patrick Bugembe, Fr. Vincent Nanseera, Fr. Anthony Zachary Rweza, Emmanuel Cardinal Wamala, Sr. Paola Caliari, Sarah Amviko, Gaetano Apamaku, Noel Ayikobua, Fr. David Baltz, Paul Aroga, Fr. Romanus Dada, Moses Atule, Prudence Joan Onen, Henry Afeku, Gabriel Adrapi, Tonny Ayoku, Emmanuel Ojok, Fr. Charles Idraku, Ambassador Maurice Kagimu Kiwanuka, Dominic Ndarhuka, Charles Sendagire, John Baptist Mpiima, Fr. Benedict Ssettuuma Jr., the late Fr. Joseph Kalyabbe, Fr. Joseph Kakooza Nyanzi, Fr. Albert Gavamuku-lya, Fr. Vincent Ssekabira, Fr. Darius Magunda, Msgr. Matthias Kanyerezi, Msgr. Charles Kimbowa, John Chrysostom Kazibwe, Lawrence Magera, Fr. Ambrose Bwangatto, Fr. Charles Ssenngando, Br. Anatoli Wasswa, Andama Richard Jferua, Moses Akuma Odims, Harun Andema, Sr. Mary Rose Nan-nyonjo, Fr. Henry Nsubuga Kiwanuka, Simon Mwebe, and Prof. Samwiri Lwanga Lunyiigo. I am grateful to all for speaking so honestly and candidly about the subjects of this book.

Whatever Fr. Ssettuuma's counsel, written primary sources also proved invaluable for this project. Rosalba Oywa graciously shared many of her unpublished writings with me. I am also deeply grateful to Fr. Sset-tuuma for sharing more than 1,000 pages of Fr. Waliggo's unpublished writ-ings, and to Mrs. Margaret Sekaaggya for sharing the annual reports of the Uganda Human Rights Commission. I also thank Fr. Charles Ssengendo and Sr. Cotilda at the Rubaga Diocesan Archives in Kampala; this archive proved especially important for my work on Cardinal Nsubuga. Ambas-sador Maurice Kagimu Kiwanuka and Jonathon L. Earle shared Benedicto Kiwanuka's extensive private papers with me; Prof. Earle also digitized the more than 6,000 documents in this collection which greatly facilitated my work. Yale University shared digital files of the *Uganda Argus* newspaper from 1955 to 1967 that proved very helpful for the chapter on Kiwanuka.

At Creighton University, I am deeply grateful to Ron Simkins and the Kripke Center for the Study of Religion and Society, the George F. Had-dix Faculty Research Fund, and the College of Arts and Sciences' Summer

Faculty Research Fellowship for generous grants that supported my field research in 2015, 2017, and 2018–19. In turn, I thank the US Fulbright Program for the nine-month grant that enabled me to complete field research on this project during my 2018–19 sabbatical.

I am grateful to the many interlocutors who provided important feedback at earlier public lectures and conference papers that informed this book: the "Le missioni in Africa: la sfida dell'inculturazione" conference, Fondazione Ambrosiana Paolo VI, Milan, Italy, September 2015; the African Studies Association annual meeting, November 2015; the American Catholic Historical Association annual meeting, January 2016; the American Society of Church History annual meeting, January 2018; Penn State University's African Studies program, January 2018; DePaul University's World Catholicism Week, April 2018; and the "Reinventing Theology in Post-Genocide Rwanda: Challenges and Hopes" conference, Kigali, Rwanda, June 2019.

In turn, I have developed the arguments in this book through previous articles in a variety of publications: "Benedicto Kiwanuka and Catholic Democracy in Uganda," *Journal of Religious History* 44, no. 2 (2020): 212–29; "Modern Roman Catholic Mission and the Legacy of Uganda's Emmanuel Cardinal Nsubuga," *International Bulletin of Missionary Research* 43, no. 2 (2019): 159–69; "The Politics of Ecumenism in Uganda, 1962-1986," *Church History* 86, no. 3 (2017): 765–95; "Uganda's Good Shepherd: The Public Witness of Emmanuel Cardinal Nsubuga, 1966–1986," *The Waliggo: A Philosophical and Theological Journal* 7.2 (2017): 23–44; "Solidarity on the Streets: Catholic Women's Leadership in Modern Uganda," in *Daughters of Wisdom: Women and Leadership in the Global Church* (Cascade, forthcoming); "Blessed Broadcast: How Uganda's Award-Winning Catholic Radio Station is Changing the Lives of its Listeners," *America Magazine* 221.4 (August 19, 2019): 28–33. In turn, Jonathon L. Earle and I will be publishing a monograph on Benedicto Kiwanuka with James Currey Press in 2021: *Contesting Catholics: Benedicto Kiwanuka and the Birth of Postcolonial Uganda*. I am grateful to all of the editors and readers who have provided critical feedback in these various forums.

Multiple colleagues reviewed and provided important suggestions on the draft manuscript or portions therein: Emmanuel Katongole, Paul Kollman, Tom Kelly, Carol Zuegner, Max Engel, George Mpanga, Herbert Busiku, and Ed Nuñez. I also thank my colleagues and students at Uganda Martyrs University during the 2018–19 academic year for the many insightful conversations that inform this book, including the animated discussions that followed my two public lectures on Benedicto Kiwanuka.

Students in my Spring 2019 "Theology of Mission and Evangelization" class at Uganda Martyrs University and my Fall 2019 "African Theology" and "Christian Tradition Global Visions" classes at Creighton University also provided very helpful feedback on several draft chapters.

I am deeply grateful to the professors and staff of St. Mary's National Major Seminary Ggaba in Kampala for hosting me during several research trips to Uganda, and for the stimulating conversations around the table that often sparked new leads and visions. In turn, I thank Jon Earle for teaching me so much about Ben Kiwanuka and colonial history in Uganda.

As always, I owe a debt of gratitude to my family. Thank you to my sister Jenny Grimes for reviewing the entire manuscript. My wife, Becky, and children, R. J., Annabelle, Samuel, and Adelaide, not only put up with my summer research trips to Africa, but they even spent a year with me in Uganda. Whatever the merits of this book, we will never forget this shared immersion as a family.

My family and I first encountered Catholic public leadership in Uganda through two priests. For my wife's family, Fr. David Baltz, MCCJ, was their lifeline to Africa. First assigned to Uganda in 1975, Fr. David went on to serve the better part of forty years as a Comboni missionary in the West Nile province of northwestern Uganda. It would be difficult to imagine a more dedicated missionary, "biking for Jesus" over thousands of miles as he conducted pastoral visits, defended villagers from marauding soldiers, and accompanied his people into exile in Congo. Like Daniel Comboni, he gave his heart for Africa. The second priest, Fr. Joseph Kakooza Nyanzi, was my supervisor during my MDiv pastoral internship in Uganda in 2004. "The Bishop of Nakasongola," as he was affectionately known, cared for Becky and me, giving us his own room for the summer and embodying compassion, humor, and an abiding faith in God's providence. A dedicated and visionary pastor, Fr. Joe has shepherded hundreds of kids through school through educational sponsorships, managed the construction of water wells, mentored countless seminarians and young priests, and spearheaded Bethany Miracle Village, a transformative effort to turn the poorest village in his parish into a model of rural education. It is to these two priests that I dedicate this book. Thank you for showing me what faithful Catholic leadership can look like on the ground in Africa.

Jay Carney
Omaha, Nebraska
September 2020

Abbreviations:
Archives, Acronyms, and Foreign Terms

ACORD	Agency for Cooperation for Research and Development (London, UK)
ACU	Archives of the Church of Uganda (Uganda Christian University Mukono and Yale University Microfilms)
ARLPI	Acholi Religious Leaders' Peace Initiative
BKMKP	Benedicto K. M. Kiwanuka Papers, Rubaga, Kampala, Uganda
Church/church	capitalized version refers to Roman Catholic Church; lower-case version refers to overall Christian community
CST	Catholic Social Teaching
DoC	Daughters of Charity (Religious nonprofit based in Uganda)
DP	Democratic Party (Political party based in Uganda)
ICS	Institute of Commonwealth Studies (University of London)
IDP	Internally Displaced People
Kabaka	king of Buganda kingdom
Katikiiro	prime minister of Buganda kingdom
KY	*Kabaka Yekka* ("The King Alone") political party
LRA	Lord's Resistance Army
Lukiiko	Buganda kingdom's parliament or legislature

NRA/NRM	National Resistance Army/National Resistance Movement
PVP	People's Voices for Peace (NGO based in northern Uganda)
RDA	Rubaga Diocesan Archives (Archdiocese of Kampala, Uganda)
UEC	Uganda Episcopal Conference (Ugandan Catholic Bishops)
UJCC	Uganda Joint Christian Council
UNLA/F	Uganda National Liberation Army/Front
UPC	Uganda People's Congress

Introduction

Leadership for God and Country in Catholic Uganda

FIGURE 1: UGANDA POLITICAL MAP

CENTRAL KAMPALA STOOD ON a knife's edge as the clock struck midnight on November 23–24, 1961. Hundreds of Catholics gathered outside the cathedral on Rubaga hill, the spiritual center of Catholicism in Uganda's

1

commercial capital. Many came with rosaries; others came armed with pan-
gas and axes. Rumors swirled that Buganda Kingdom officials had arrested
Archbishop Joseph Kiwanuka of Rubaga, the preeminent Catholic leader in
Uganda.[1] Earlier that day, Archbishop Kiwanuka released his pastoral letter, "Church and State: Guiding Principles." The letter came in the run-up
to the 1962 national elections and anticipated independence from Britain;
it also came in the midst of the Buganda government's crackdown against
Catholic supporters of the Democratic Party, a nationalist party that had
called for Buganda's *kabaka* (or king) to become a constitutional monarch
in a unified Uganda. In his letter, Archbishop Kiwanuka protested the political harassment of Catholics and predicted that "when political parties are
established in a country, if the king still mixes up in politics, the kingship is
on the way to digging its own grave."[2] Before releasing the letter, Kiwanuka
left the country for a fundraising trip in the USA, and his Vicar General
Fr. Emmanuel Nsubuga was on a pastoral visit outside the city. So in their
places, Buganda officials arrested Msgr. Joseph Ssebayigga, parish priest of
Rubaga Cathedral and spokesperson for the Archdiocese of Rubaga. After
hours of interrogation and brief imprisonment, Msgr. Ssebayigga was released in the early morning hours of November 24. The Catholic crowd's
hymns of protest turned into hymns of thanksgiving, but many still wanted
to march to the *kabaka's* palace at nearby Mengo. Rushing back from his
pastoral visit, Msgr. Nsubuga played an instrumental role in calming the
crowd. Ultimately Catholics marched not to Mengo to protest their *kabaka*,
but to the nearby Marian shrine at Nalukolongo to pray for peace.[3]

Four and a half years later, a very different scene unfolded on Rubaga
hill and its environs. Although Prime Minister Milton Obote and Buganda
Kabaka Edward Muteesa II had been allies during the 1962 elections, they

1. Buganda kingdom comprises the south-central region of modern-day Uganda,
including the capital city of Kampala. In the nineteenth century, Buganda was the most
powerful kingdom in the territory that later became Uganda. British colonial officials
developed the neologism "Uganda" from a Swahili mispronunciation of Buganda, and
the former title was applied to the entire Uganda Protectorate in 1900. The "Baganda" are
the people of Buganda; "Luganda" is the language. Similar etymological patterns apply to
Uganda's other ethnic groups.

2. Joseph Kiwanuka, "Church and State," sec. 27. In Uganda this letter remains the
most famous Catholic political statement; successive archbishops of Kampala issued 40th
and 50th anniversary statements in 2001 and 2011. As I discovered, it is also the only
Ugandan pastoral letter on sale in Paulines Bookstore, the largest Catholic bookstore in
Kampala.

3. This account draws on "Kabaka Orders"; Kimbowa, *Emmanuel Cardinal Kiwanuka
Nsubuga*, 40–43; Mukasa, "Day Kabaka Muteesa," 9.

became fierce rivals by 1966. After a near-putsch by pro-*kabaka* cabinet members in February 1966, Obote declared a state of emergency, coincidentally on the same day as Archbishop Kiwanuka's death. Three months later, Buganda's provincial legislature, the *lukiiko*, announced that it would no longer recognize the Uganda federal government's sovereignty on Buganda soil. On May 25, 1966, Obote sent in the national army, under the command of Col. Idi Amin Dada, to destroy the *kabaka's* residence at Mengo Palace and arrest or kill Muteesa. After a daylong firefight, the *kabaka's* militia was defeated, and over 2,000 lay dead. Muteesa himself barely escaped by climbing over the walls of his burning palace and taking refuge in the nearby Catholic priests' rectory on Rubaga hill. One of these priests was none other than Fr. Emmanuel Nsubuga. Muteesa advised Nsubuga—soon to be named the new Archbishop of Kampala—to help "look after Buganda" until he could return in the future. Nsubuga and his confreres then dressed the *kabaka* as a priest and arranged transport for him to the Rwandan border and into exile.[4]

Principles and Profiles of Catholic Social Leadership in Uganda

These two anecdotes from the beginning of Uganda's independence period capture the tension embodied in the title of this book. "For God and My Country" is Uganda's official motto, similar to the "In God We Trust" motto found on American currency. When Uganda's Catholic bishops write pastoral letters, they end them with these words. The motto reflects Uganda's deep religiosity as well as religious leaders' commitment to collaborating with the state in service to the common good, a good framed in the nation-state terms so ubiquitous in the modern era. And yet for all of the collaboration of church and state, the strictures of Acts 5:29 have not disappeared in Uganda—church leaders have often determined that "we must obey God rather than any human authority," especially in times of political oppression where churches have been among the last bulwarks of independence.

The churches' relative political autonomy stems from their social influence in a deeply religious country.[5] Uganda is an overwhelmingly Christian country, with 85 percent of the population identifying as Christian. For its

4. Wasswa, interview. On Kabaka Muteesa's "entrusting" of Buganda to Emmanuel Nsubuga and Anglican Bishop Dunstan Nsubuga, see Ward, "Church of Uganda Amidst Conflict," 76.

5. The best overview of the Christian churches' public impact in postcolonial Uganda remains Gifford, *African Christianity*, 112–80.

part, the Catholic Church is the single largest Christian church in Uganda, comprising over 40 percent of the population.[6] The Catholic Church runs the nation's largest network of health facilities, including an unmatched rural network of dispensaries and clinics, thirteen health training schools, and thirty-two hospitals.[7] As of 2015, the Ugandan Catholic Church was also running over 5,400 primary and secondary schools, nearly 150 vocational schools, five universities, and twenty-eight major and minor seminaries.[8] The Church also plays an integral role in rural development, emergency relief, and poverty eradication through Caritas, the official Church agency for social development, and Centenary Bank, the largest microfinance bank in Uganda. In turn, the Ugandan Catholic Church exemplifies the broader trend on the African continent, where in 2010 the Catholic Church operated over 33,000 primary schools, 10,000 secondary schools, and 16,000 health centers. In Paul Gifford's words, "No other single agency on the continent can rival this contribution."[9]

In turn, the ethical and theological foundation of the Ugandan Church's extensive social outreach rests in the modern tradition of Catholic social teaching (CST). Initiated in 1891 through Pope Leo XIII's encyclical *Rerum Novarum* on the labor question in industrial Europe, the CST tradition has developed intellectually through a series of papal and other magisterial statements. It has been incarnated in social movements and organizations such as Catholic Action, *Caritas*, *Pax Christi*, Catholic Relief Services, and the Pro-Life movement. CST draws on the theological riches of the Christian tradition to serve the common good, defined at Vatican II as "the sum total of social conditions which allow people, either as groups or as individuals, to reach their fulfillment more fully and more easily."[10] It is based on the fundamental conviction that human beings are relational and social by nature. In the words of the *Compendium of the Social Doctrine of the Church*, "Man, in fact, is not a solitary being, but a 'social being,' and unless he relates himself to others he can neither live nor develop his

---

6. Kollman and Toms Smedley, *Understanding World Christianity*, 112.

7. This includes two hospitals widely seen as among the nation's best—Uganda Martyrs Lubaga and St. Francis Nsambya, both located in Kampala. Statistics are from 2015 (Nassuuna, "Catholic Health Services in Uganda," 206, 208).

8. Okello, "Catholic Founded Primary and Secondary Schools," 138.

9. Gifford, *Christianity, Development and Modernity*, 90.

10. Second Vatican Council, *Gaudium et Spes*, sec. 26.

potential."[11] The Church thus encourages the broadest possible community participation, balancing personal rights with social responsibilities.

There is no dogmatic list of the essential principles or themes of Catholic social teaching. However, most commentators agree that the foundational principle of the tradition is the dignity and sanctity of human life created in the image of God (Gen 1:28). Defending human dignity entails protecting life from conception to natural death and publicly safeguarding a variety of other human rights, including "food, housing, work, education and access to culture, transportation, basic health care, the freedom of communication and expression, and the protection of religious freedom."[12] Other common CST principles include the priority of the family. The CST tradition sees families—rather than individuals or social groups—as the core building blocks of communities. Going back to *Rerum Novarum*, CST supports legal protection of private property rights, yet the tradition also relativizes this right within the broader principle of the "universal destination of goods"—namely that "all created things should be shared fairly by all mankind under the guidance of justice tempered by charity."[13] CST emphasizes the dignity of labor, including workers' rights to a living wage, free association, and the formation of unions. Under the influence of Latin American liberation theology, CST in the latter half of the twentieth century developed a growing concern for addressing the structural causes of poverty, building solidarity with the poor, and encouraging integral human development (see for example Pope Paul VI's *Populorum Progressio* [1967] and Pope John Paul II's *Sollicitudo Rei Socialis* [1987]). During the nuclear age of the Cold War, CST emphasized the connection between justice and peace, shifting from a predominantly just-war posture to a more pacifistic approach encouraging nonviolent alternatives and addressing the root causes of violence (see Pope John XXIII's *Pacem en Terris* or the US Bishops' 1983 encyclical, *The Challenge of Peace*). In the twenty-first century, environmental concern has risen to the fore, as evidenced in Pope Francis's 2015 encyclical *Laudato Si'*.

In addition to edited collections of the CST documents themselves, there is an ample body of theological analysis of the principles of Catholic

11. Pontifical Council of Justice and Peace, *Compendium of the Social Doctrine*, sec. 110.

12. Pontifical Council of Justice and Peace, *Compendium of the Social Doctrine*, sec. 166.

13. Pontifical Council of Justice and Peace, *Compendium of the Social Doctrine*, sec. 171, quoting *Gaudium et Spes*, sec. 69.

social teaching.[14] To make a genuine public impact, however, CST requires not just the enunciation of principles, but the implementation and translation of these ideas into specific cultural and political contexts. This in turn requires nuanced, prophetic, and persevering leadership.

Located at the intersection of Ugandan church-state relations and the CST tradition, this book presents six case studies in Catholic leadership in postcolonial Uganda. Each chapter is framed around a particular person(s) and theme, and each closes by synthesizing key lessons in Catholic public leadership. Convinced that American Christians can learn from their brothers and sisters in Africa, I intentionally frame these chapters dialogically between Uganda and the American context within which I live and work. Although each chapter can be read on its own, and each contains its own distinctive takeaways, the chapters build on each other, following a roughly chronological development from the 1960s to the 2010s. In this sense, reading the book sequentially will enable the reader to gain a deepened understanding of the history, public theology, and sociopolitical influence of Uganda's Catholic Church in the late twentieth and early twenty-first centuries. To echo the Ugandan theologian Emmanuel Katongole, the book explores the "social performance" of Catholicism through a biographical lens as these stories played out on the "rough ground" of late twentieth- and early twenty-first-century Uganda.[15] The chapters are organized around the following leaders and themes:

Prime Minister Benedicto Kiwanuka: The Catholic Politician

A devout Catholic from a peasant background, Benedicto K. M. Kiwanuka helped found and lead the Catholic-dominated Democratic Party in the late 1950s and early 1960s. He facilitated Uganda's transition from British colonial rule to self-government as Chief Minister in 1961–1962. He remained a vigorous opponent of his successor Milton Obote's growing

---

14. See Massaro, *Living Justice*; Matzko McCarthy, *Heart of Catholic Social Teaching*.

15. "Performance" is a prominent theme throughout Katongole's extensive theological corpus, reflecting his overriding emphasis on the importance of narrative or story for shaping theological and social imagination. Katongole's hope is for Christianity to become a more determinative story shaping social performance in Africa. "But this way of thinking about politics in Africa also provides a way to view Christianity as itself a form of politics, a unique performance grounded in a different set of stories that shape unique expectations and characters" (Katongole, *Sacrifice of Africa*, 3). Katongole draws the language of "rough ground" in part from the philosophical work of Ludwig Wittgenstein.

authoritarianism, leading Obote to imprison him between 1969 and 1971. Released after General Idi Amin Dada's *coup d'état* in January 1971, Kiwanuka was appointed as the first Ugandan Chief Justice of the Supreme Court. He fell afoul of Amin over a judicial dispute and was kidnapped and murdered in September 1972. He is widely seen in Uganda as a martyr to democracy and the rule of law. Shaped by key currents of Catholic social thought in the 1950s and 1960s, he is the most important Catholic politician in modern Uganda. To this day, he remains the only Ugandan prime minister or president to peacefully hand over power to a democratically elected successor. For all of his achievements, Kiwanuka has been criticized for his dogmatic, uncompromising politics of "truth and justice" that some critics trace to his deep Catholic convictions.

Emmanuel Cardinal Nsubuga: The Shepherd of the People

Following in the illustrious footsteps of Archbishop Joseph Kiwanuka, Cardinal Nsubuga served as Archbishop of Kampala between 1966 and 1990. He led the Church through the most brutal years of the Amin dictatorship (1971–1979) and the post-Amin civil war during Obote's second government (1981-85). He is remembered locally for his ecumenical outreach, solidarity with the poor, and courageous public witness during years of suffering, violence, and oppression. Nsubuga has been the subject of a local biography but is virtually unknown outside of Uganda. Controversies remain over whether he and the Ugandan Catholic Bishops' Conference should have written more publicly on Amin's abuses during the 1970s, following the lead of Archbishop Janani Luwum, the outspoken Anglican prelate assassinated by Amin in 1977.

Fr. John Mary Waliggo: Uganda's Liberation Theologian

Fr. Waliggo was the most important Catholic scholar and public theologian in postcolonial Uganda. A noted historian of early Catholic missions in Uganda, Waliggo wrote voluminously on social ethics and theology and became a political activist in the late 1970s and 1980s. Forced into exile on two separate occasions under Amin and Obote, he influenced many of the Church's most important pastoral letters on political themes. He later served as secretary to the constitutional revision process that culminated with the promulgation of the 1995 constitution, and he helped guide

Uganda's National Human Rights Commission from its founding in 1996 until his death in 2008. Like the Cameroonian Jesuit Jean-Marc Éla and many other theologians in South Africa and Latin America, his theological vision was strongly shaped by the concept of integral liberation. His close relationship with the ruling National Resistance Movement government in the 1990s and 2000s remains a point of contention, and his witness also raises the question of how involved Catholic priests should become in politics and public life.

Sr. Rose Mystica Muyinza: Solidarity on the Streets

A childhood convert to Catholicism, Sr. Muyinza entered the Little Sisters of St. Francis in the 1950s before leaving the congregation in the 1960s to labor as a social worker with street children. Continuing to embrace the identity and lifestyle of a Catholic sister, she founded a nonprofit organization in Kampala called "Daughters of Charity." In the 1980s and 1990s, she worked extensively with vulnerable women, widows, and orphaned children in the midst of civil war and the HIV-AIDS crisis. Dubbed the "Mother Teresa of Uganda," Sr. Rose is an important symbol of the crucial public contributions of Catholic women's religious in Uganda and of the broader Ugandan Catholic Church's massive efforts in social charity and development work. The later demise of her community raises important questions concerning administration, leadership style, and the relationship between Catholic NGOs and the institutional church.

Fr. Tonino Pasolini and Ms. Sherry Meyer:
Missionaries of the Media

An Italian priest of the Comboni Missionaries of the Heart of Jesus, Pasolini first came to Uganda in 1966. Meyer, an American from Indiana, arrived in 1991 as a Catholic lay missionary. In addition to their extensive pastoral and catechetical work, they are best known for inaugurating Radio Pacis, winner of the 2007 BBC award for best new radio station in Africa. Headquartered in Arua in the northwestern West Nile province, Radio Pacis reaches a listening audience of ten million in five different languages across three countries. The station provides Catholic, local, and international news, religious programming, and community engagement with the goals of encouraging "gospel values" in society and building understanding across religious and ethnic lines. *Radio Pacis* reflects the critical role of Catholic media in modern public life in Uganda, and Pasolini and Meyer also provide insight into the controversial question of whether and how to be postcolonial Western missionaries in Africa.

Mrs. Rosalba Ato Oywa: Mama Peace

A lay Catholic activist from Gulu, Mrs. Oywa lost family members and nearly her own life during the early days of the northern Uganda war in 1986–1987. This inspired her to join the NGO staff of the Agency for Cooperation and Research in Development (ACORD), where she served as one of the lead analysts on northern Uganda. As a member of the Gulu Women's Development Committee, she organized a famous 1989 women's march that briefly halted the violence. She later collaborated with the Refugee Law Project to publicize inhumane conditions in northern Uganda's IDP camps, and she also founded a local NGO, People's Voice for Peace. She is a prominent example of both the women's activists and religious leaders who have championed the cause of peace in northern Uganda in the face of both government abuses and the LRA's own twisted religious fanaticism.

Whatever its title, this book does not attempt to offer an encyclopedic overview of Catholic leadership in modern Uganda. One could make convincing arguments for the inclusion of other well-known Catholic figures not profiled in these pages. Some are omitted due to the book's focus on the postcolonial period. The aforementioned Archbishop Kiwanuka or the missionary Bishop Henri Streicher were important Catholic figures during the British colonial period, but my primary focus here is on the postcolonial era since 1962.[16] In turn, several prominent contemporary figures such as Archbishop John-Baptist Odama and Sr. Rosemary Nyirumbe, both based in Gulu, have been the subjects of recent studies.[17] In contrast, one of my goals in this book is to raise awareness of important Ugandan Catholic leaders who are not as well-known outside the country. Ultimately, my selections here are illustrative. Subjects were chosen based on their exemplification of key themes in the Catholic Church's modern public witness and

16. On Archbishop Kiwanuka, see Waliggo, *Man of Vision*. On Streicher, see Shorter, *Cross and Flag*, 49–50, and Hastings, *Church in Africa*, 565–66.

17. On Nyirumbe, see Katongole, *Born from Lament*, 134–42, and Scaperlanda, *Rosemary Nyirumbe*. On Odama's spiritual vision, see Katongole, *Journey of Reconciliation*, 121–36.

social teaching, such as peacebuilding, the preferential option for the poor, integral liberation, and democratization.[18]

Amidst the diverse witness of these leaders, several core arguments course through this book. First, the leaders profiled here share a holistic, liberative, and humanitarian approach to their grassroots apostolates in service to religiously pluralistic societies and the common good, broadly reflecting core principles of Catholic social teaching and the social mission of the Second Vatican Council of Vatican II (1962–65). Second, echoing Uganda's national motto, "For God and My Country," these leaders' public apostolates entailed a twofold commitment to both the church and the nation, a delicate balancing act that involved seeking public influence and retaining working relationships with state leaders, yet also striving to maintain political independence. Third, all of these leaders work within institutions, yet often find themselves pushing up against institutional boundaries, whether of church, state, or society. In this sense, they embody a restless and often stubborn commitment to "respond and belong to the gap,"[19] to allow the gospel to explode the thick, intractable walls of politics and economics that resist the gospel and marginalize the poor. In this sense, eschatological vision—especially faith in Christ's resurrection and God's overall providence—helped these leaders to persevere in the midst of some of the darkest periods of Ugandan history, echoing the christological text of John 1:5: "A light shines in the darkness, and the darkness has not overcome it." Finally, these leaders' public apostolates demonstrate how the Church can be a sacrament given for the life of the world, embodying Vatican II's call for the Church to be "a sign and instrument of communion with God and of unity among people."[20] In other words, the Church points not to itself but to the "already-but-not-yet" reign of God inaugurated in the mission and ministry of Jesus Christ. Yet faithful service on behalf of the world necessitates a deep grounding in spirituality, sacrament, and Catholic practice. Like figures such as Joseph Cardinal Bernardin of the USA, Archbishop Oscar Romero of El Salvador, or Mother Teresa of Calcutta, these Ugandan leaders demonstrate that, at its best, deepened Catholic religious identity will lead to a broader "catholic" commitment to the whole world.

18. I should add that I hope this work might inspire Ugandan researchers and other Global South scholars to conduct further research and writing on the many deserving Christian leaders who should be better known outside their own local contexts.

19. Katongole and Rice, *Reconciling All Things*, 125.

20. Second Vatican Council, *Lumen Gentium*, sec. 1.

FIGURE 2: CATHOLIC DIOCESES OF UGANDA

Why Catholic Uganda?

The book's delineation around Catholic Uganda raises three interlocking questions. First, why conduct a national rather than regional or continental study of African Catholicism? Second, why should Uganda be the locus of such a study? Third, what led me as an American outsider to undertake this project?

On the first question, the general scholarly tendency in African theology and social ethics has been to focus on "Africa." One thinks here of the titles of influential recent works such as Diane Stinton's *Jesus of Africa*, Emmanuel Katongole's *The Sacrifice of Africa*, or Agbonkhianmeghe E. Orobator's *The Church We Want: African Catholics Look to Vatican II*. The ubiquity of such "Africa" nomenclature has many roots, including postcolonial theology's embrace of African inculturation, the analytical success of the pan-African ideal, and, frankly, publishers' need to sell books.[21] However, this trend can also occlude the historical, political, and cultural diversity of the continent. Nigeria, South Africa, the Democratic Republic of the Congo, Kenya, and Egypt are all very different places. Or as I sometimes make my American students chant in class, "Africa is a continent, not a country." The fields of African theology and African social ethics would benefit from thicker, more situated studies that recognize that Christian expression is always deeply local.[22]

At the same time, the Church is "catholic," or universal, and Ugandan Catholicism is not sealed off on an island. So although the geographic framing here is that of Uganda, Uganda does not exist in a vacuum. This juxtaposition of the local and the global is even more important for a religious tradition like Catholicism that balances centralization and unity with universality and diversity in expression, or what Morier-Genoud calls "the Catholic motto [of] difference in unity."[23] This productive synergy between the local and the global is also evident in the lives of several of the leaders profiled here. Benedicto Kiwanuka and John Mary Waliggo were deeply shaped by their years studying in the UK; Sr. Rose Muyinza raised most of the money for her social welfare projects through international fundraising networks in Italy, the UK, and the USA; Tonino Pasolini and Sherry Meyer were born and raised in the West and continue to straddle two worlds as international missionaries.

On the second question, historically Uganda was one of the most important foundations of Catholic Christianity in Africa. Home of the first burgeoning Catholic missions in late nineteenth-century Africa, Uganda became perhaps the most influential center for Catholic Christianity in colonial Africa. Rooted in the witness of the famous Buganda (later Uganda) Martyrs of the 1880s, spurred by competition with Anglicans, and propagated by multiple missionary congregations, the Catholic Church became

21. This trend is not just limited to North American publishers. Paulines Publications Africa, the leading Catholic publisher in Africa, almost exclusively publishes books with a continental or regional focus.

22. To be sure, such situated studies do exist, but they tend to be academic monographs in African history and the social sciences (e.g., Martin, *Catholic Women of Congo-Brazzaville*; Morier-Genoud, *Catholicism and the Making of Politics*; Foster, *African Catholic*). African church history and missiology have included both sweeping continental studies (e.g., Hastings, *Church in Africa*; Sundkler and Steed, *History of the Church in Africa*; Baur, *2000 Years*) and more contextual monographs (e.g., Sanneh, *Translating the Message*; Kollman, *Evangelization of Slaves*; Carney, *Rwanda Before the Genocide*).

23. Morier-Genoud, *Catholicism and the Making of Politics*, 173.

Uganda's largest religious community in the early twentieth century, a status it has retained to the present day. In 1939, the Holy See appointed Ugandan priest Joseph Kiwanuka as the first sub-Saharan African Catholic bishop in modern times, and his Diocese of Masaka became the first African diocese fully entrusted to indigenous clergy. It was Uganda that became host to the first papal visit to Africa, where in 1969 Pope Paul VI famously declared, "You may, and you must, have an African Christianity."[24] More recently, the Uganda Martyrs Shrine has become the preeminent pilgrimage destination in Africa. In 2019, more than 2 million pilgrims journeyed to Namugongo for the June 3 feast day of the Uganda Martyrs. In this regard, Catholicism is not just important within Uganda; Ugandan Catholicism has also been the most influential Catholic "brand" in East Africa as a whole.

Finally, let me share a word on my own personal journey toward writing this book. I am not a Ugandan, nor was I raised, educated, or missioned in Uganda. However, Uganda has been a part of my life for many years. I first lived in the country in 2004, completing a teaching and ministry internship in rural Nakasongola as a part of my MDiv studies at Duke University. Here I worked with Fr. Joseph Kakooza Nyanzi, a man who first demonstrated for me the transformative social leadership impact of the "African priest." Although my subsequent doctoral research focused on neighboring Rwanda, I returned to Uganda multiple times over the next fifteen years, most recently as a US Fulbright scholar based at Uganda Martyrs University during the 2018–2019 academic year. This recurring personal experience has given me firsthand knowledge of the country and helped me to build the oral networks that inform much of my analysis in this book. I have also had the privilege of working with outstanding local research assistants in Uganda such as George Mpanga, Herbert Busiku, and Alex Kimpi. To be sure, I do not and cannot write as a Ugandan insider, and there are real limits to any foreign researcher's ability to grasp the nuances of local culture, politics, language, social relations, or even the quotidian dimensions of church life. Yet in the words of one Luganda proverb, *omugenyi yakulaga ewatonya*—"it is the visitor who shows you a leaking part of the house."[25] My hope is that even with my epistemological and existential limitations, I still offer fresh insights and accurate and balanced analysis of the leaders profiled herein. In turn, I am convinced that these leaders offer

24. Orobator, *Theology Brewed in an African Pot*, 131.

25. I am grateful to Fr. Benedict Ssettuuma for sharing this proverb with me.

important pastoral lessons not just for Ugandans, but also for American Christians and other people of good will around the world.

Whatever my own experience, this book does not assume that readers possess in-depth familiarity with Ugandan church or state history. Before moving into the main content chapters, then, I will conclude this introduction with a brief overview of the historical roots of the Catholic Church in Uganda, especially in Buganda kingdom, as well as a brief overview of postcolonial political history in Uganda. Those who are well-versed in these subjects are welcome to proceed straight to the first chapter.

Catholic Roots in Buganda and Uganda

FIGURE 3: UGANDA'S TRADITIONAL KINGDOMS AND TERRITORIES

Catholic and Anglican missionaries first arrived in Buganda kingdom in the 1870s. In the late nineteenth century, Buganda was the most powerful kingdom in the wider territory that would later become Britain's Uganda Protectorate. Other major polities and people groups in precolonial

Uganda included Bunyoro, Buganda's main military rival to the northwest; Toro kingdom bordering the western Rwenzori mountains; Ankole in the southwest; Busoga in the south-central area near modern-day Jinja; Teso and Karamoja in the east; and Acholiland in the north. In general, northern and eastern groups were pastoralists with Nilotic languages and relatively decentralized polities; southerners and westerners shared Bantu languages and more hierarchical, centralized political systems. Traditional religion included the concept of a high God such as the Baganda's *Katonda* or the Banyankole's *Ruhanga*, but daily religious practice focused on maintaining harmony with ancestors and spirits through the intercessory power of mediums and sacrificial offerings at sacred shrines.[26] In Buganda kingdom, the king, or *kabaka,* was a prominent spiritual figure in his own right. In Richard Reid's words, "political leadership necessitated intimate connections with the divine and the transcendent."[27]

Not surprisingly, early Christian missionaries in Uganda found their ostensibly spiritual project intricately interwoven with webs of political power. Their very presence in Uganda stemmed from an 1876 invitation from Buganda's *kabaka*, Muteesa I, passed through the hands of the British-American explorer Henry Morton Stanley.[28] Protestant missionaries from the British Church Missionary Society, led by the Scottsman Alexander Mackay, duly arrived in 1877–78. French Catholic missionaries from the Missionaries of Africa or White Fathers, led by Fr. Simeon Lourdel, followed in February 1879. By the end of 1879, these religious rivals were engaged in a sometimes-bitter struggle to win the allegiances of Muteesa, a king who seemed alternately intrigued and perplexed by their intra-Christian theological disputes.[29] Having previously welcomed Islam into Buganda in the 1860s, Muteesa now seemed to lean toward the Catholics, although he never formally joined any of these ostensibly foreign religions.[30]

26. Leeming et al., *History of East Africa*, 72. See also Ray, *Myth, Ritual and Kingship in Buganda*; p'Bitek, *Religion of the Central Luo*. One should be careful on making wide assumptions; p'Bitek, for example, argues that the Luo had no concept of a high God.

27. Reid, *History of Modern Uganda*, 169.

28. Karugire, *Political History*, 52.

29. Catholic-Anglican relations were by no means uniformly hostile in these early years. Catechumens frequented both missions, and even European missionaries co-existed and at times enjoyed amicable relations (see Tourigny, *So Abundant a Harvest*, 24; Waliggo, "Catholic Church in the Buddu Province," 22.)

30. On Muteesa's earlier embracing of Islam, his persecution of Muslims in the 1870s, and the historical legacies of Muslim-Christian tensions in Buganda, see Rowe, "Islam

Frustrated with royal intransigence and the social challenge of polygamy, the White Fathers and the CMS missionaries in 1882 left Buganda for Bukumbi, located on the south side of Lake Victoria in modern-day Tanzania. Far from collapsing, the Christian missions they left behind grew in their absence. Muteesa died in 1884 and was succeeded as *kabaka* by his 18-year-old son, Mwanga. Although the new king had frequented the Christian missions in the early 1880s, he became increasingly suspicious of his young Christian pages or attendants, especially their religious zeal, independence, moral obstinacy, and foreign connections.[31] In late 1885 and 1886, he ordered the execution of incoming Anglican Bishop James Hannington and initiated a persecution of his Christian court pages. Between November 1885 and January 1887, over 100 died, including twenty-three Anglicans and twenty-two Catholics who were canonized by their respective churches as first the "Buganda Martyrs" and later the "Uganda Martyrs."[32]

Ultimately Mwanga's Christian repression was more capricious than systematic. Christian numbers continued to grow, especially among the younger generation of royal pages and future chiefs. In September 1888, Anglican, Catholic, and Muslim leaders joined forces to topple Mwanga. A year later, Christian chiefs rallied together to fight Mwanga's Muslim successor, Kabaka Kalema.[33] Ecumenical collaboration did not last long, however, and by 1890–1891 Catholic and Protestant chiefs were engaged in a fierce struggle to control the political future of Buganda. Ultimately, the British East Africa Company, represented by Frederick Lugard, fifty Sudanese soldiers, and an automatic maxim or machine gun, resolved the conflict in favor of the Anglican chiefs. In 1892–1893, the losing Catholic chiefs were exiled to the southwestern region of Buganda known as Buddu.[34] In 1894, Great Britain established a protectorate over the region and

under Idi Amin," 267–79.

31. In Buganda, court pages were the future chiefs; hence the political sensitivity of their religious commitments.

32. For a helpful summary of the Martyrs, see Kollman and Toms Smedley, *Understanding World Christianity*, 37–39, 243–46. The classic Catholic account is Faupel, *African Holocaust*. On the political dynamics of the martyrdoms, see Waliggo, "Catholic Church in the Buddu Province," 34–37; Twaddle, "Emergence of Politico-Religious Groupings," 81–92; Kassimir, "Complex Martyrs," 357–82.

33. Rowe, "Islam under Idi Amin," 270–72.

34. On the Buddu exile, see Waliggo, "Catholic Church in the Buddu Province," 50–54.

further empowered Protestant chiefs through suppressing an 1897–99 rebellion led by Mwanga and Kabalega, the king of neighboring Bunyoro.[35]

The 1900 Buganda Agreement established long-term British colonial authority in Uganda with a semi-established Anglican Church. Mwanga's three-year-old son, Daudi Chwa, was named *kabaka* under the regency of Apollo Kaggwa, the Anglican *katikiiro,* or prime minister. Most of Buganda's twentieth-century political elites and all of its *kabakas* would be Anglicans. Even though Buganda counted more Catholics than Anglicans, Catholic counties received 37 percent of land versus the 61 percent allocated to Anglican counties.[36] Anglicans thus stood at the apex of the colonial political hierarchy, followed by Catholics, Muslims, and adherents of traditional religion. Despite this relative discrimination, Catholic leaders retained generally cordial relations with British colonial officials, especially since they depended on the state for most of their educational resources.[37] A good example here comes from the 1916 pastoral instructions of Buganda's longtime Vicar Apostolic, the White Father Bishop Henri Streicher, in which Streicher praised the British protectorate for introducing to Uganda "liberty of conscience, abolition of slavery, suppression of barbarous customs, justice, and creation of private property."[38] To summarize, although the Catholic Church was by no means persecuted by British authorities, the Anglican Church occupied an "unofficial privileged position" in Uganda throughout the colonial era.[39] A lingering sense of political marginalization would remain a key marker of Ugandan Catholic identity throughout most of the twentieth century.

The lack of formal political power was not without its advantages, however. Freed from the responsibilities and baggage of explicit colonial partnership, the Ugandan Catholic Church focused on evangelization, education, pastoral ministry, and indigenizing its leadership. In front of a crowd of 15,000, Bazilio Lumu and Victor Mukasa Womeraka were

---

35. For further background, see Low, *Buganda in Modern History*, 27–50; Karugire, *Political History*, 68–95.

36. Earle, *Colonial Buganda*, 183.

37. In Hansen's words, "At a time [after World War I] when the question of nationality was paramount, the Catholic missions clearly felt themselves to be in a weak position in view of their multi-national corps of missionaries. In order to show loyalty they had to be accommodating to the state on which they depended for their educational resources" (Hansen, "Colonial State's Policy," 169).

38. Streicher, "Appel à la charité," 119. The translation from the French is mine.

39. Hansen, *Mission, Church, and State*, 28.

ordained in 1913, the first African Catholic priests in sub-Saharan Africa in the modern era.[40] By 1915, Uganda had the largest Catholic population in all of Africa with an estimated 135,000 converts.[41] In particular, Buddu province—located around the city of Masaka in the southwestern region of Buganda kingdom—became the Catholic spiritual nerve-center of southern Uganda. Catholics established a strong, almost theocratic subculture in Buddu, and during the interwar period Masaka became the first African Catholic diocese to be led by indigenous clergy. As Waliggo has argued, Buddu Catholicism was notable for its strongly Marian and sacramental spirituality, with a heavy emphasis on moral discipline and heroic witness.[42] As in much of the rest of sub-Saharan Africa, the Catholic Church became especially known for its work in healthcare and education. The church also benefitted from visionary leadership. Bishop Streicher led the Buganda church for over three decades and prioritized the indigenization of Catholic clergy. Streicher started a major seminary in 1903 and championed the cases of Lumu and Womeraka, famously stating, "To get one indigenous priest is for me more important than to convert ten thousand people."[43] He ultimately achieved both goals. When Streicher retired in 1933, the Ugandan Catholic Church counted over 300,000 Christians, forty-six African priests, and 280 religious sisters.[44]

Not surprisingly, in 1939 Buganda provided the Catholic Church its first sub-Saharan African bishop in the person of Joseph Kiwanuka of Masaka. Born in 1899, the "man of nines" was ordained a priest in 1929, and in 1939 he was named as the first black African Catholic bishop in modern times. You could also call Kiwanuka a "man of firsts." With Fr. Timoteo Ssemogerere, he was the first Ugandan to earn a doctorate in canon law in Rome in 1932, graduating with highest honors.[45] He also was the first Ugandan to become a White Father priest. After being named a bishop, he

40. Kollman and Toms Smedley, *Understanding World Christianity*, 250. On the history behind these June 1913 ordinations, see Waliggo, *History of African Priests*, 27–57.

41. Kollman and Toms Smedley, *Understanding World Christianity*, 55.

42. Waliggo, "Catholic Church in the Buddu Province," 75. See also Tusingire, *Evangelisation of Uganda*, 90–96.

43. Kollman and Toms Smedley, *Understanding World Christianity*, 228–29.

44. Hastings, *Church in Africa*, 565. On Streicher's pastoral vision in the context of the early White Father missions in Africa, see Shorter, *Cross and Flag in Africa*. On the history of Uganda's Catholic priesthood and especially Katigondo Major Seminary, see Waliggo, *History of African Priests*.

45. Tourigny, *Century of Trials and Blessings*, 55.

was given stewardship over the diocese of Masaka, the first canonical territory to be handed over exclusively to indigenous clergy.[46]

After his appointment to Masaka, Kiwanuka began to enunciate a more activist political role for the Catholic bishop. In a 1947 pastoral letter, he initiated church-based economic cooperatives and styled himself as the "educator of the nation," offering moral guidance to the people while respecting what he called the "legitimate autonomy" of secular political leaders. "I have discovered that the leadership people want me to exercise in the country is not political as such, but rather leadership of offering good and wise education, which will help our nation and put it on the right track. In such responsibility I can be a leader without necessarily annoying the political rulers."[47] During the so-called "Kabaka Crisis" of 1953–55, Kiwanuka emerged as a key player in negotiations to bring Kabaka Edward Muteesa II back from British-imposed exile in London. At the Namirembe Conference of 1954, he spoke strongly in favor of both Buganda's and Uganda's self-determination, yet he also enunciated a more apolitical role for the *kabaka* as a constitutional monarch. In his words, "Buganda is anxious to place the *Kabaka* outside the storm of politics which caused the present crisis."[48] He would echo and deepen these sentiments—to much more controversial effect—in his 1961 pastoral letter, *Church and State: Guiding Principles*, as discussed at the beginning of this introduction.

Although I have been speaking primarily about Buganda, the Catholic Church also grew extensively in western, eastern, and northern Uganda throughout the early twentieth century. British and Dutch missionaries of the St. Joseph's Missionary Society, popularly known as the "Mill Hill Fathers," were most influential in Kampala city and parts of eastern Uganda, such as Teso and Bukedi. Their most important legacy was in education, especially through influential Kampala schools like Namilyango College and St. Peter's Nsambya.[49] In contrast, the Italian Verona Fathers or Combonis were the dominant male missionary congregation in the north (see chapter

---

46. Controversy remains over why Kiwanuka was not named as the first African Cardinal. Instead, Tanzania's youthful Laurean Rugambwa was the first African given the cardinal's hat in 1961. Off the record, several Ugandan scholars attributed this to lingering missionary resentment toward Kiwanuka's nationalist instincts and willingness to challenge missionary paternalism and racism (author's field notes, Kampala, Uganda, June 2015).

47. Quoted in Waliggo, *Man of Vision*, 25.

48. "J. Kiwanuka Statement," 175.

49. O'Neil, *Mission to the Upper Nile*, 22, 50, 92.

5). Some of Uganda's largest Catholic populations grew up in northern regions such as Nebbi in West Nile and Gulu in Acholiland, and Comboni devotions such as the Rosary and the Sacred Heart became mainstays of Catholic practice.[50] Like the White Fathers and the Mill Hill missionaries, the Combonis were agents of social development and education, and by the late colonial period they were encouraging Catholics to be actively involved in the political process.

Like the Anglican Church of Uganda, then, the Catholic Church during the colonial period became a national church that crossed ethnic and linguistic lines (not always without tensions). In fact, by the time of independence in 1962, the Catholic Church was Uganda's largest religious community, and leaders like Archbishop Kiwanuka were major players in the public realm. The leaders profiled in this book—including Archbishop Kiwanuka's friend, Benedicto Kiwanuka, and successor, Archbishop Emmanuel Kiwanuka Nsubuga—built on this legacy.[51] They did not do so in a political vacuum, however. Before turning to these postcolonial leaders, let me briefly sketch Uganda's political leadership and history since independence.

Postcolonial Politics in Uganda

Archbishop Kiwanuka's *Church and State* letter was released in the immediate run-up to independence in 1962. Earlier in 1961, Benedicto Kiwanuka's Democratic Party (DP) had triumphed in national legislative elections boycotted by many of Kabaka Edward Muteesa's royalist allies in Buganda (chapter 1). After the 1961 victory of the DP, traditionalist Baganda came together to start the *Kabaka Yekka* ("Kabaka Alone") party. In October 1961, KY formed an unlikely alliance with Milton Obote's nationalist Uganda People's Congress (UPC) with the express purpose of defeating the DP in national elections in April 1962. They achieved this goal, and Obote succeeded Kiwanuka as prime minister before Uganda's accession to independence in October 1962.

Obote served as prime minister and later president of Uganda between 1962 and 1971. An Anglican and ethnic Langi from northern Uganda, Obote had the unenviable task of building a nation out of Uganda's forty

50. Whitmore, *Imitating Christ in Magwi*, 58.

51. Despite their eponymous names, these three prominent Catholic Kiwanukas were not directly related.

disparate tribes, tribes whose identities had been politically instrumental-ized through the British colonial policy of indirectly ruling through custom-ary authorities. Obote struggled in particular with Buganda's unwillingness to enter fully into a unified Ugandan state; this tension culminated with the 1966 Battle of Mengo discussed at the beginning of this chapter. Al-though a civilian himself, Obote became more dependent on the military as the 1960s progressed, and his UPC party bought off, marginalized, or banned the political opposition. Obote's refusal to hold elections after 1962 undermined his popular credibility, especially in Buganda, which was also subject to a state of emergency during the final five years of his rule. At the same time, the 1960s were a period of relative prosperity, development, and nation-building in Uganda. A close ally of Tanzania's Julius Nyerere, Obote mirrored Nyerere's socialist turn with his "move to the left," embodied in his Nakivubo Pronouncements of 1970.[52]

Before Obote could implement this new economic vision, however, General Idi Amin Dada, his erstwhile ally and head of the military, over-threw him in a *coup d'état* on January 25, 1971. Amin's populist charm won him many early admirers. Notably, he reached out to religious leaders within a week of the coup, proclaiming that he "feared no man on this earth apart from God" and would respect religion more than the mildly secular Obote.[53] Amin was especially cheered among the Baganda, who had never forgiven Obote for forcing Kabaka Muteesa out of the country and placing Buganda under a state of emergency.[54] In late 1972, Amin expelled Uganda's Indian population. Although popular with the Ugandan masses—Asians had cultivated African resentment through their longtime domination of commerce and business—this decision significantly undermined Uganda's economy throughout the rest of the 1970s. At the same time, a failed 1972 invasion led by Obote and other Ugandan exiles sparked a major crack-down on perceived political dissidents, and Uganda descended into an orgy of political violence in which an estimated 300,000 died (chapter 2). Amin's rhetorical gifts and theatrical flair kept him in the international

52. For an appreciative analysis of Obote's legacy, see Ingham, *Obote*. For a much more critical account, see Mutibwa, *Buganda Factor*.

53. Low, "Uganda Unhinged," 219, 226–27.

54. Edward Muteesa died under suspicious circumstances in London in November 1969; many suspected Obote's agents in his death. Obote did not allow Muteesa's body to be flown back to Uganda for traditional burial, further alienating the Baganda. Amin's decision to bring the Kabaka's body back to Uganda in March 1971 thus won him further plaudits.

limelight, but by the end of the decade his regime was bankrupt, kept in power through Libyan loans and violent state repression.

After an ill-fated invasion of northern Tanzania in October 1978, Amin drew international opprobrium from all quarters. In April 1979, he fled Uganda just ahead of the invading United National Liberation Front (UNLF), a coalition of Ugandan exiles backed by Nyerere's Tanzanian army. Uganda cycled through three prime ministers over the next eighteen months, and the UNLF military controlled developments from behind the scenes. With the support of the military, Milton Obote returned from exile in May 1980. The Democratic Party, led by Benedicto Kiwanuka's former deputy, the Catholic Paul Ssemogerere, very likely won December 1980 elections, but the electoral commission ruled Obote and the UPC as winners.[55] In early 1981, multiple rebel movements sprung up against Obote, including Yoweri Museveni's National Resistance Army (NRA). The "Obote II" regime responded with a crackdown on perceived opponents of all stripes, and Uganda descended into a scorched earth civil war that would prove even more violent than the blood-soaked Amin years, especially in West Nile and the "Luweero Triangle" of central Buganda.[56] Although Obote's economic management was much better than that of Amin, the civil war and his lack of electoral legitimacy caught up to him. In July 1985, Obote was again overthrown by his army, this time led by the Acholi generals Tito Okello and Bazilio Okello. However, the Okello brothers' regime lasted only six months before Museveni's NRA took over Kampala and the government in January 1986.

For more than thirty years, Museveni has pulled the strings of political power in Uganda and, for that matter, much of eastern and central Africa. During his first decade in power, his no-party National Resistance Movement (NRM) enjoyed widespread grassroots popularity and instituted welcome political reforms, culminating with the promulgation of the 1995 Constitution (chapter 3). In addition to substantial investment in infrastructure, Museveni and the NRM also proved to be successful economic reformers. Uganda's GDP has consistently grown at over 6 percent per annum since the late 1980s, and the poverty rate declined from 56 percent to

---

55. Nabudere, "External and Internal Factors," 302–3.

56. On the post-Amin political transition of 1979 to 1981 and the Luweero war of 1981 to 1985, see Kasozi, *Social Origins of Violence*, 132–82. Kasozi estimates that upwards of 300,000 died during Amin's regime and more than 500,000 during Uganda's civil war (4).

31 percent during the first two decades of NRM rule.[57] Politically, though, Uganda under Museveni has become what Aili Tripp describes as a "semi-authoritarian" regime.[58] Although the government agreed to the reintroduction of a multiparty system in the mid-2000s, and although Uganda's judicial courts and media retain some independence, the NRM has utilized increasingly repressive means to stay in power. Crackdowns on the political opposition have been especially brutal, particularly in the runups to national elections. State violence was also resisted and resented in northern Uganda in the context of the LRA insurgency which dominated the region in the 1990s and 2000s (chapter 6). Museveni and the NRM retain a chokehold on legislative and executive power, and the Parliament and courts have dispensed with the constitutional term limits and age limit clauses that might have pushed Museveni into retirement. At the time of writing, the opposition shows signs of uniting around the figures of Kizza Besigye, four-time presidential candidate and leader of the Forum for Democratic Change, and the musician Robert "Bobi Wine" Kyagulanyi and his youth-dominated "People Power Movement." January 2021 presidential and parliamentary elections thus promise to be hotly contested.

It is on this political and social backdrop that the seven Catholic leaders profiled in this book operated from the 1960s to the 2010s. It is to their stories, and the leadership lessons therein, that we now turn.

---

57. Tripp, *Museveni's Uganda*, 2.

58. Tripp, *Museveni's Uganda*, 3–5.

The Catholic Politician

Benedicto K. M. Kiwanuka

THE CHIEF JUSTICE OF Uganda's Supreme Court had just entered his chambers to read through an overview of the day's cases. It was a Thursday in September 1972. Benedicto K. M. Kiwanuka arrived at Uganda's High Court straight from Catholic Mass at Rubaga Cathedral, a ritual in which he partook on a daily basis. A week earlier, he had taken the unusual step of requesting and receiving the Catholic sacrament of anointing, a ritual only granted in cases of serious illness or in anticipation of death. As Kiwanuka sat in his chambers, a commotion ensued. Plains-clothes intelligence officers with Uganda's General Security Unit confronted and arrested him. As he was forcibly removed from the building, he shouted in Luganda to one of his assistants, "*Matiya bantutte, naye abaana ba Maria tebafa!*" ("Mathias, they have taken me, but children of Mother Mary do not die!").[1] These were the last public words of Benedicto Kiwanuka. To this day, his body has not been recovered.

One of the most important political leaders of the independence era, Benedicto Kiwanuka is largely unknown outside of Uganda. (His grandson, Matthias Kiwanuka, the former New York Giants defensive end and two-time Super Bowl winner, has far greater name recognition in my own United States). But as Uganda's first chief minister and the architect of

1. This account is taken from: "Bendicto Kagimu Mugumba Kiwanuka"; Kiwanuka, "Address." Accounts of Kiwanuka's death can also be found in the Uganda Judiciary Ethics Board's September 2018 issue of *The Judiciary Insider*, an issue that was largely dedicated to Kiwanuka's memory.

the Democratic Party's rise to power between 1959 and 1962, Kiwanuka was one of the key players in Uganda's transition from British colonialism to national independence. Even more significantly, he remains the only Ugandan prime minister or president to peacefully hand over power to a democratically elected successor. The most influential Catholic politician in modern Uganda, Kiwanuka embodied an eclectic mix of sometimes-competing identities: a devout and traditional Catholic layman, an anti-colonial African nationalist, and a politician for whom democracy was a sacred cause. His brutal death at the hands of Amin also led many to see him as a martyr to the rule of law and judicial independence, and his family and friends are now pushing the Archdiocese of Kampala to introduce his cause as a "patron saint of Ugandan politicians."[2]

Kiwanuka's witness highlights the important if controversial question of what it means to speak of a "Christian" or "Catholic" political leader in the modern world. Such questions are fraught with ambiguities. The devout politician can overly assume God's will, claiming that God has directly spoken to him and personally called him to lead the country into the promised land. On the other extreme are the Christian politicians who wholly privatize and compartmentalize their own religious faith. In the USA, the most famous example of this trend was John F. Kennedy who, in part to fend off Protestant fears of his own Catholic identity, claimed that "I believe in a President whose religious views are his own private affair."[3] Another challenge is the sheer breadth of the Catholic Church's political and social teachings in service to the common good, defined at Vatican II as the "sum total of those conditions of social living which allow people, either as groups or as individuals, to reach their fulfillment more fully and more easily."[4] In the modern world, those teachings include standing up for religious freedom and human rights, supporting democratization and civic education, exercising a preferential option for the poor, caring for the environment, welcoming migrants, and advocating for the sanctity of human life from conception to natural death. But rare is the Catholic politician who is fully conversant with this tradition, much less one who embraces a range of positions that cut across the liberal-conservative ideological spectrum that dominate American politics in particular.

2. "Bendicto Kagimu Mugumba Kiwanuka," 13.

3. Kennedy, "Address to the Greater Houston Ministerial Association," 4:31–4:36.

4. Second Vatican Council, "*Gaudium et Spes*," sec. 26.

FIGURE 4

So, although the Church in both Africa and America often laments the dearth of truly "Catholic" politicians, the task may be harder than we imagine. Benedicto Kiwanuka is by no means a perfect model. In the words of the Ugandan historian Samwiiri Lwanga Lunyiigo, "no politician is a saint!"[5] But Kiwanuka's witness can teach us about what it could mean to see politics as a vocation in the modern world. In particular, I will emphasize four dimensions of Kiwanuka's political witness: 1) his commitment to building the common good and popular political participation through democratic systems, 2) his uncompromising stand against injustice and oppression, 3) his embodiment of public Catholic witness as a martyr, and 4) his ability to model personal Catholic devotion without political sectarianism.

Benedicto Kiwanuka's Biography[6]

Benedicto Kagimu Mugumba Kiwanuka was born in May 1922 in Buddu province, the historic heartland of Catholicism in Buganda (see introduction). His father, Fulgensio Musoke, was a minor village chief, but in

5. Lwanga Lunyiigo, interview.

6. This biographical section draws on Bade, *Benedicto Kiwanuka*; "Bendicto Kagimu Mugumba Kiwanuka"; Earle, *Colonial Buganda*, 197–207.

Buganda's hierarchical culture he was classified as a *mukopi,* or peasant. He was also an alcoholic who squandered his family's limited property and wealth, dying in 1940 in relative penury from complications of gonorrhea. In the words of Kiwanuka's biographer, Albert Bade, his father's demise led Kiwanuka to "develop a permanent dislike for extravagance, polygamy and poverty."[7]

Like nearly all aspiring Catholic youth in Buddu, Benedicto pursued primary education in a church-sponsored school. In his case, he enrolled at Villa Maria Primary School in Masaka district, one of the first schools started by the White Fathers. He went on to pursue secondary school studies at St. Peter's Nsambya, a prominent Kampala secondary school run by the Mill Hill Missionaries. After his father's bankruptcy and death, however, Kiwanuka could no longer pay his school fees, and he withdrew from St. Peter's in 1941. Shortly thereafter, he enlisted in the King's African Rifles, Britain's colonial regiment in East Africa. Over the next four years, he trained in Kenya and then served in Egypt and Palestine, working first as a warrant officer and clerk before rising to the rank of sergeant-major.[8] Like many young African men of his generation, this wartime experience broadened his cultural and intellectual horizons.[9] After leaving the army in 1946, Kiwanuka returned to Uganda where he met Maxensia Zulbango, a devout Catholic who had also studied at the White Fathers' school at Villa Maria. Maxensia's family was from Bunyoro, Buganda's fierce precolonial rival. Demonstrating the stubbornness for which he would later be famous (or infamous), Kiwanuka refused to yield to family opposition to this inter-ethnic relationship. Maxensia had wanted to become a nun, but Kiwanuka's determined courtship and written eloquence convinced her to marry him in 1947.[10]

Post-war work as an assistant librarian in Kampala's High Court piqued Kiwanuka's interest in law. By 1950, he had raised sufficient funds from Catholic clergy and friends to enroll in pre-law studies at Pope Pius XII Catholic University in Basutoland (present-day Lesotho). Kiwanuka excelled in his coursework, earning the accolades of Catholic staff in the process. Commending Kiwanuka's plans to enroll in law at the University

7. Bade, *Benedicto Kiwanuka,* 2.

8. "Appendix B to Gen Order 1100 of 1944"; "Bendicto Kagimu Mugumba Kiwanuka," 2.

9. See Parsons, *African Rank-and-File.*

10. Regina Kiwanuka, interview.

of London, one Pius XII professor framed Kiwanuka's future work in terms of a Catholic vocation to public service: "But keep on! Africa needs men who shall give her a social and political organisation thoroughly inspired by the message of Our Lord as interpreted by His Vicar on earth, Our Holy Father the Pope."[11] In part due to the financial assistance of Archbishop Joseph Cabana of Rubaga and Bishop Joseph Kiwanuka of Masaka, Kiwanuka commenced law studies at the University of London in 1952. Here he became involved with the Uganda Students Association and other anti-colonial, pan-African movements based in London. Kiwanuka also became close to Buganda's king, Kabaka Edward Muteesa II, during the latter's exile period in London between 1953 and 1955.[12]

Kiwanuka finished his UK law studies in 1956 and came back to Uganda to practice law. He returned in the immediate aftermath of the disputed 1955 election of Buganda's *katikiiro* (or prime minister), a closely contested race between the Anglican Michael Kintu and the Catholic Matayo Mugwanya. Kintu's election—in part due to Kabaka Muteesa and his Anglican advisors' refusal to countenance the election of the Catholic Mugwanya as *katikiiro*—further galvanized the Catholic leaders of the nascent Democratic Party (DP), who publicly launched their party in August 1956. Kiwanuka joined the DP in 1958, and in August of that year he succeeded Mugwanya as the party's president-general. Several months later, he was elected to represent Buddu in Buganda's *lukiiko*.

Over the next two and a half years, Kiwanuka positioned the DP as an anti-communist, anti-colonial nationalist movement. Toward this end, he moved to expand the DP's base beyond its Catholic core to include both Anglicans and Muslims. As he wrote in *Uganda Argus* in 1958, "Come ye all. Come ye Muslims, Protestants, pagans, Catholics. Come to our camp. Join in this great struggle to bring light to the people of this country."[13] He and his subordinates constructed a strong party organization outside of Buganda, building particular strength in such far-flung regions as West Nile and Ankole. Under their motto of *amazima n'obwenkanya*, or "Truth

11. Rector of Pius XII College, correspondence.

12. Kabaka Muteesa was deported to London in November 1953 for his refusal to accede to British colonial governor Andrew Cohen's aim to incorporate Buganda into a federal Uganda and a possible regional East African Federation. Mass protests and extensive political negotiations ultimately led to his return to Buganda in 1955 as a constitutional monarch whose political ambitions had not abated.

13. "D. P. Leader's Appeal," 2. The quote also demonstrates Kiwanuka's embracing of modernization and desire to move Uganda away from its traditional roots.

and Justice," the DP presented itself as the champions of Uganda's peasants regardless of ethnic or religious background.[14] In Buganda, the DP made the politically risky decision to oppose separate independence for Buganda kingdom, advocating instead for a more unitary system of postcolonial government marked by universal suffrage and direct elections.

Kiwanuka and the DP came to power through February 1961 national elections in which the party competed on near-even terms with the Uganda People's Congress (UPC) nationwide and scooped up nearly all of the votes of the 3.5 percent of Baganda who participated (most Baganda boycotted the election on the *kabaka's* orders). At age thirty-eight, Benedicto Kiwanuka, a Ganda Catholic commoner, became chief minister, the most powerful elected African leader in Uganda. In these final days of colonial rule, Britain controlled economic policy, the judicial courts, foreign policy, and security, so Kiwanuka's hands were tied during his brief thirteen months in power. He had more influence over issues such as agriculture, health, education, and transportation, and he made headway on Africanizing the civil service and raising prices for coffee and cotton growers. Political fortunes soon turned against the DP, however. To defeat the DP, the UPC formed an alliance of convenience with the Baganda traditionalists of the Kabaka Yekka (KY) party, and the latter conducted a massive campaign of political intimidation against the DP during the electoral period of February 1962 to April 1962. Between January 1 and December 20, 1962, there were no fewer than 639 offenses committed against DP supporters, 498 of which were prosecuted and 306 of which resulted in convictions.[15] This violence had its desired effect; Kiwanuka and the DP lost both February 1962 *lukiiko* elections in Buganda and April 1962 national elections across Uganda. It was the UPC's Milton Obote, rather than Ben Kiwanuka, who welcomed Uganda's independence as prime minister in October 1962.

Kiwanuka assumed the role of *de facto* opposition leader for the rest of the 1960s. Even as the UPC courted and ultimately poached some of his fellow DP leaders, Kiwanuka refused to compromise. He wrote publicly and passionately against Obote's economic policies as well as his suspension of the constitution in February 1966.[16] He later spoke out against the indefinite

14. Earle notes the innovative nature of the term in post-war Catholic discourse. The Luganda phrase *amazima n'obwenkanya* conveyed a sense of "calling Christians to attend to the travail of a weaker person or disenfranchised citizens," emphasizing the connection between social justice and social stability (Earle, *Colonial Buganda*, 190).

15. Inspector General of Police, correspondence to Benedicto Kiwanuka.

16. Kiwanuka, correspondence to Milton Obote, March 3, 1966 and May 20, 1964.

extension of Buganda's state of emergency and the overall transformation of Uganda in the late 1960s into an authoritarian, military-backed, one-party regime.[17] In 1969, he refused entreaties by his erstwhile political ally E. M. K. Mulira to merge the DP with the UPC, rhetorically asking how he could join a president and party known for its "corruption, tribalism, vandalism, squandering of public funds, political cowardice, and exploitation of the masses by those on top."[18] Kiwanuka's vocal opposition led the government to arrest him on two occasions in late 1969, including after the near-assassination of Obote in December 1969.[19] Their party banned, Kiwanuka and other DP leaders languished in prison for over a year.

Kiwanuka's liberator was the unlikely figure of Gen. Idi Amin, the Ugandan military chief whose resignation Kiwanuka had demanded back in 1964 on account of Amin's trafficking in gold in neighboring Congo. Whatever his past disputes with Amin, Kiwanuka welcomed any alternative to Obote by 1971. In a politically astute act, Amin released Kiwanuka and other Ganda political prisoners. Days after his release, Kiwanuka wrote a fawning letter to Amin, describing him as "God's agent" and claiming that "by your successful overthrow of the Obote regime you have saved the country from totalitarianism, tyranny, corruption, and nepotism."[20] The rapprochement between Amin and Kiwanuka culminated with Amin's June 1971 decision to appoint Kiwanuka as the first Ugandan Chief Justice of the Supreme Court. Kiwanuka and Amin were seen in public on many occasions in 1971 and early 1972, and Kiwanuka invited the president to share Christmas dinner at his house.

This entente was not to last, however. Fearful of Kiwanuka's political popularity and unable to manipulate him on judicial matters, Amin gave a speech in August 1972 in which he lambasted a "small pocket of people in Masaka District who were in the pockets of the outgoing Asians and the imperialists and were thus opposed to the move to expel them . . . including one with a very high position in the government."[21] Kiwanuka was the obvious target here, as he himself pointed out in a letter to Amin on August

17. Kiwanuka, "DP Response to State of Emergency."

18. Kiwanuka, correspondence to E. M. K. Mulira. Mulira proposed this merger in the aftermath of Pope Paul VI's visit to Kampala in August 1969, arguing that the pope's visit opened up new "vistas" of cooperation between erstwhile rivals within the churches and political parties.

19. "Detention Notice."

20. Kiwanuka, correspondence to Idi Amin Dada, February 4, 1971.

21. "All Asians Must Go," 1.

31.[22] In September, Amin's government arrested and detained the British businessman Daniel Stewart without warrant or trial. The British High Commissioner appealed to Kiwanuka to intervene in the case. Kiwanuka agreed, further enraging Amin.[23] Rumors of Kiwanuka's impending arrest swirled through Kampala's political circles. Despite the urgings of his wife, friends, and Catholic Archbishop Emmanuel Nsubuga, Kiwanuka refused to flee into exile. As he allegedly commented to his friend, Fr. Clement Kiggundu, "We cannot allow our country to continue in this way because we too are threatened. If we have to die, let's die as martyrs rather than as cowards."[24]

Kiwanuka was arrested on September 21, 1972, as recounted at the beginning of this chapter. After public outcry including a call from Kenyan President Jomo Kenyatta, Amin privately offered Kiwanuka his freedom if he would publicly blame Obote for his arrest. Never one to take the path of convenience over principle, Kiwanuka refused. According to some eye-witness reports, Amin then shot him twice in the face.[25] His death came early in a wave of political assassinations, including prominent Ganda Catholics such as Joseph Mubiru, the president of Uganda's National Bank, and the aforementioned Fr. Kiggundu, the editor of the influential Catholic newspaper *Munno* who was killed in January 1973 in part for his investigations into the circumstances surrounding Kiwanuka's death.[26] Uganda descended into a reign of terror that would linger throughout Amin's rule in the 1970s.[27]

Kiwanuka the Catholic Politician

After offering this overview of Kiwanuka's life, let us now consider the nature of Kiwanuka's personal Catholic identity and the ways in which his

22. Kiwanuka, correspondence to Idi Amin Dada, August 31, 1972.

23. Bade, *Benedicto Kiwanuka*, 156.

24. Kiwanuka, quoted in Bade, *Benedicto Kiwanuka*, 158.

25. Maurice Kagimu Kiwanuka, "Address." Maurice Kiwanuka's view is plausible and reflects years of investigation, but there is no clear consensus on the manner of Ben Kiwanuka's death or the final location of his remains.

26. Mwebe, interview. Mwebe worked as a journalist under Kiggundu and succeeded him as editor of *Munno*. He was also active in DP politics at various points of his career. Bade also thinks Kiggundu was killed due to his connections to Kiwanuka (Bade, *Benedicto Kiwanuka*, 160).

27. See Kyemba, *State of Blood*, and Kasozi, *Social Origins of Violence*.

Catholic faith and Catholic theology shaped his political thought. Given Kiwanuka's own consistent opposition to his opponents' labeling of the DP as a "Catholic party," how exactly can we describe Kiwanuka as a "Catholic politician?"

First, Kiwanuka was a devout Catholic on a personal level. Not only was he educated by the White Fathers, but he shared their devotion to the Virgin Mary, once advising his brother to "always blend your studies with the devotion of the rosary."[28] As a youth, Kiwanuka's surrogate father was Fr. Benedicto Nsubuga, one of Uganda's first indigenous priests who served in the local parish at Villa Maria. Later as a university student, Kiwanuka became involved with Catholic student groups, and he was a frequent subscriber to Catholic book services. As an adult, he attended daily Mass where he frequently served the altar, continuing this practice even as Chief Minister and later Chief Justice. He was known for carrying his Catholic missal or daily prayer book in public, a rarity among nonclergy of his or any age. Kiwanuka maintained close relations with the Catholic hierarchy in Uganda; his son, Maurice Kagimu Kiwanuka, described Uganda's first African Archbishop, Joseph Kiwanuka, as the "decisive influence" on his father.[29] Even as a politician, Kiwanuka did not shy away from theological debate. Shortly before his death, Kiwanuka engaged in an erudite argument with a Catholic priest and theology professor at Makerere University who was advocating for a married priesthood. Kiwanuka took a conservative line in this debate, reminding the priest that his vows of obedience required him to honor church law and praising what he described as the "totalitarianism which has kept the Church intact all of these 2,000 years."[30] On a personal level, then, Kiwanuka's Catholicism was deeply held, fervently practiced, and trended toward the traditional.

Beyond his personal devotion, Catholic intellectual and social thought also exerted significant influence on Kiwanuka. In addition to the standard

28. Bade, *Benedicto Kiwanuka*, 3–4.

29. Maurice Kiwanuka, interview.

30. Kiwanuka, correspondence to Aloysius Lugira. The full quote reads as follows: "This totalitarianism in the Catholic Church was not introduced to it by man. It started with Our Lord himself. He always spoke as a man with authority (Mark 1:27). He commanded and condemned. He accepted no compromise . . . It is this totalitarianism which has kept His Church intact for all of these 2,000 years." Whatever their differences on married clergy, Lugira later endorsed Kiwanuka's canonization cause and praised Kiwanuka's contributions to Uganda's social development (Lugira, "Catholic Church and Development").

political theory of thinkers like Locke and Rousseau, Kiwanuka, during his London law studies, was a voluminous reader of the nineteenth-century British Catholic theologian John Henry Newman. Newman reinforced Kiwanuka's commitment to the primacy of proclaiming truth. For example, in his annotated notes on Newman's autobiography *Apologia Pro Vita Sua*, Kiwanuka highlighted Newman's claims that "the first of virtues is to tell the truth and shame the devil" and that "silence is also absolutely forbidden to a Catholic, as a mortal sin . . . when it is a duty to make a profession of faith."[31] Likewise, one of Kiwanuka's advisors was Fr. Tarcisio Agostoni, an Italian Comboni missionary from northern Uganda, who was the most important advocate of Catholic social thought during Uganda's independence era.[32] It was Agostoni who suggested the DP's emblem of "T" (Truth) and "J" (Justice) set on the background of a rising sun over Uganda. To quote Agostoni in a 1959 letter to Kiwanuka, "So the D.P. will be the life for the country, the heat (and the love); will provide for economics and industry; is the one to awaken people from the sleep and to open their eyes as the sun in the morning."[33] This Catholic-themed motto of "Truth and Justice" would remain the DP credo long after Kiwanuka's death.

At the same time, Kiwanuka could also be quite critical of foreign missionaries and settlers alike. In a fascinating exchange during his London student years, Kiwanuka wrote a blistering letter to the missionary rector of Bukalasa Seminary for insinuating that he was a "communist." Here Kiwanuka castigated Catholic missionaries for jeopardizing the Church's future in Uganda due to their intransigence in the face of rising African nationalism. In Kiwanuka's words, "Are you a missionary come to Africa to preach the Gospel of the Lord—the Brotherhood of Man?—or a political agent to suppress nationalism?"[34] In 1954, he wrote to the *U.K. Catholic Herald* newspaper to counter a British settler's opposition to the return of Kabaka Muteesa. Here Kiwanuka argued that, as a foreigner, his European Catholic interlocutor did not have the right to demand special privileges. "She should understand [that] she has less title to such rights than that of the devils who cried out in rage in Carpharnaum [*sic*] of Galilee."[35]

31. Newman, *Apologia Pro Vita Sua*, 225 (annotation).

32. See Agostoni, *Every Citizen's Handbook*.

33. Agostoni, correspondence to Benedicto Kiwanuka, July 8, 1959.

34. Kiwanuka, Correspondence to Rector of St. Thomas Seminary, August 17, 1953.

35. Kiwanuka, Correspondence to Editor of *Catholic Herald*, February 27, 1954. Kiwanuka here is referencing the biblical story of Jesus' curing of a Capernaum demoniac

Thus, if Kiwanuka wore his Catholic devotion on his sleeve, he was also a political nationalist. His nationalism explains everything from his opposition to missionary colonialism in the early 1950s to his refusal to countenance Ganda separatism in the early 1960s to his determination to Africanize the Ugandan civil service during his brief tenure as Chief Minister.[36] To be fair, his nationalism was shaped by the DP's original purpose to enfranchise and empower Uganda's large Catholic population. Yet he also fought to broaden DP's image and membership beyond the party's sectarian roots. Kiwanuka confessed that he was an "ardent" Catholic, but "I am not a bigot. I cherish Christian principles because I am convinced that they are the best for human society . . . Let us suffice to say that our principles in the Democratic Party are based on the idea of tolerance and fair play."[37] And as he wrote after the April 1962 elections,

> In all seriousness I can say here and now that the Democratic Party is NOT and has never been a 'Catholic' Party . . . A Party cannot survive on one religion alone in a country such as ours . . . It is not good to base one's political thought on one's religion because once this is done the person concerned will not stop there but will cultivate a tendency to religious intolerance.[38]

In this regard, Kiwanuka reflected and even anticipated one of the core shifts in modern Catholic social teaching, namely that Catholic politicians should fight for the common good—and especially the needs of the poor and marginalized—rather than simply advocate for Catholic institutional interests. This spirit is perhaps best captured in the opening words of Vatican II's final 1965 document, *Gaudium et Spes*: "The joys and the hopes, the griefs and the anxieties of the men of this age, especially those who are poor or in any way afflicted, these are the joys and hopes, the griefs and anxieties of the followers of Christ. Indeed, nothing genuinely human fails to raise an echo in their hearts."[39] For his part, Kiwanuka did not try to recreate the "Catholic Party" movement of early twentieth-century Europe, parties explicitly founded to defend institutional Catholic interests in the public sphere. Rather, the DP reflected the more ecumenical "Christian Democratic" movement in post-war Italy or Germany—democratic, nationalist,

in Mark 1:21–28.

36. "Democratic Party 13-Point Programme."

37. Kiwanuka, "Uganda Elections–1962," 42.

38. Kiwanuka, "Uganda Elections–1962," 4.

39. Second Vatican Council, *Gaudium et Spes*, sec. 1.

formally secular, anti-communist, and hovering between the center-left and center-right.[40] One also sees resonance with the theologically tinged yet formally secular nationalism of Tanzania's Julius Nyerere, a devout Catholic and the most successful nationalist politician in postcolonial East Africa who was recently named a "Servant of God," the first step on the road to Catholic sainthood. Like Nyerere, Kiwanuka presented his party not as a Catholic empowerment movement but rather as a vanguard empowering working-class *bakopi* or common peasants. Toward this end, DP policies included free primary education, industrialization and agricultural development, road and infrastructural development, private-sector loans, and respect for private property rights.[41] The DP's manifesto also included women's empowerment, including voting rights, property inheritance, and expanded higher education, and critics would later accuse the party of encouraging a disruptive gender egalitarianism in both the public and private spheres.[42]

In particular, Kiwanuka's and the DP's religious-cum-political zeal was directed toward advocating for genuine democracy. For Kiwanuka, all major political decisions should be subject to direct voting, whether the issue concerned the adoption of a federal versus unitary system of government, the composition of the head of state, or, most controversially, elections for Buganda's representatives to the national legislature.[43] Commitment to direct elections was a "cardinal principle in a democracy," equivalent for Kiwanuka to a theological dogma such as Christ's divinity, as he expressed to Anglican Archbishop of Canterbury Geoffrey Fisher in their testy exchange of October 1961.[44] Kiwanuka's commitment to genuine democratization was also one of the primary reasons he continued to reject communism

40. On the transitions from "Catholic parties" to "Christian democracy" movements, see Buchanan and Conway, *Political Catholicism in Europe*; Horn, *Western European Liberation Theology*; Kaiser, *Christian Democracy*. Kiwanuka also sought funding from several Christian Democratic parties in Europe in 1960 ("From Bonn to (British) Foreign Office").

41. "Democratic Party 13-point Programme"; "Democratic Party Manifesto."

42. Akwacha, "You Cannot Have Two Masters."

43. Kiwanuka, "Views on Forms." It was for this principle of direct elections that Kiwanuka fell on his sword at the September 1961 London Constitutional Conference, paving the way for the Uganda People's Congress/Kabaka Yekka partnership that would usher Uganda into independence. (Kiwanuka, "What Happened in London," 1–2).

44. Kiwanuka, Correspondence to Geoffrey Fisher. Kiwanuka repeatedly pinpointed Fisher's intervention as a key turning point in the London negotiations (Kiwanuka, "Uganda Elections–1962," 9–18).

and financial support from the USSR and China.[45] In a moment of prophetic prescience in 1962, he expressed his trepidations for the future of Ugandan democracy "if after the next General Election another Party which is not this one got into power here."[46] If Ghana's Kwame Nkrumah famously encouraged his followers to "seek ye first the political kingdom,"[47] Kiwanuka's political theology ultimately revolved around popular sovereignty and national self-determination. Riffing on Matthew's Sermon on the Mount, the DP manifesto "Forward to Freedom" best captured what Kiwanuka saw as his party's mission to support democratization and self-government: *"BLESSED ARE THEY WHO STRUGGLE AND TOIL FOR THE SAKE OF SELF-GOVERNMENT FOR THEY WILL HAVE EVERLASTING SELF-SATISFACTION IN A SELF-GOVERNING UGANDA."*[48] As with the aspirational vision of the Sermon on the Mount, the dream of functional democratic self-government would remain an elusive one for Kiwanuka and his fellow DP prophets.

Conclusion: Kiwanuka's Leadership Legacies

In summary, then, we can highlight several key legacies of Ben Kiwanuka as a Catholic political leader in modern Uganda. First, he was genuinely committed to building the common good and broader public participation through the establishment of democratic systems and the rule of law. He recognized the dangers of a political world in which personal charisma and the force of military arms can easily trump democratic structures. After leaving power, he was consistent in his opposition to injustice and oppression, his calls for parliamentary elections, and his denunciation of the melding of party and state under Obote and the UPC. As Chief Justice, he stood for the rule of law and promised to protect Ugandans against government abuses, "not allowing you to be thrown into prison at the whims of an Executive."[49] He ultimately paid for his convictions with his life. In many ways Kiwanuka was prescient; his worries that dominant political parties would not respect democratic norms have proven true. Nor have

45. Kiwanuka, "DP Presidential Address 1959."

46. Kiwanuka, "Presidential Address," 3.

47. Quoted in Hastings, *History of African Christianity*, 86.

48. "Democratic Party Manifesto," 12 (emphasis original). Here Kiwanuka is reworking Jesus's beatitudes in Matthew's Sermon on the Mount (Matt 5:1–12).

49. Kiwanuka, "Address at International Conference Center," 7.

Kiwanuka's successors followed his example of gracefully leaving office. Nearly sixty years after he stepped down, Kiwanuka remains the only Ugandan leader to peacefully hand over power to a democratically elected successor from the opposition party.

Second, Kiwanuka offers a witness of personal Catholic devotion without public sectarianism. He was devout, principled, loyal to the Catholic hierarchy, and had no dint of personal scandal. Kiwanuka's thought and writings are peppered with theological and biblical references. He shared the theistic vision of most of his contemporaries, including a broader role for religion in public life than what might be deemed acceptable in modern America. Yet he recognized the dangers of religious or political discourse that excludes, ostracizes, or separates people into "us" and "them" categories. A good example of this blending of theistic rhetoric with an inclusive politics comes from Kiwanuka's prayer at the 1959 DP Annual Conference that "our Blessed Lord give us His guidance in our deliberations," seeking Christ's guidance to support DP's own version of the four freedoms: "freedom of worship, freedom of movement, freedom of speech, and above all freedom of thought."[50] Unlike his fellow Catholic politician, Gregoire Kayibanda, in Rwanda, Kiwanuka did not use violence or mobilize a social group to take power based solely on their demographic advantage.[51] Rather, he tried to build a broadly based coalition across ethnic and religious lines. In a twenty-first-century political world that continues to struggle with how to bridge divisions of race, religion, gender, and ethnicity, the breadth of Kiwanuka's vision comes as a breath of fresh air.

Third, Kiwanuka's reputation was that of a stubborn, incorruptible advocate for "truth and justice." As his old mentor Fr. Agostoni wrote in 1971, Kiwanuka's new job as Chief Justice of the Supreme Court better fit his "honesty," "sense of righteousness," and "uncompromising sense of religion" than the "tortuous labyrinth of politics."[52] On the negative side, his "rigidity" and deep sense of personal righteousness bordered on arrogance, making it difficult for him to make political allies, engage in the typical horse-trading of politics, or see the potential errors of his own ways. In turn, DP critics and even sympathizers have charged that Kiwanuka's martyr-like

---

50. Kiwanuka, "DP Presidential Address 1959," 3, 5. This echoes the "four freedoms" speech of Franklin D. Roosevelt in his 1941 State of the Union address.

51. Kayibanda led the Parmehutu political party to victory in the 1961–62 elections, castigating the minority Tutsi as the oppressors and enemies of the majority Hutu (see Carney, *Rwanda Before the Genocide*, 135–39).

52. Agostoni, corrrespondence to Kiwanuka, July 4, 1971.

personality made it impossible for the DP to ever actually assume political power; the party would rather die on the barracks of truth and justice than make the compromises necessary in the hurly-burly of state politics. In this regard, Kiwanuka reflects Max Weber's "ethic of ultimate ends" that values principles above all else, in contrast to an "ethic of responsibility" in which political leaders must prudently act within the political limits of their time in light of the "foreseeable results of one's action."[53] He also symbolizes the ambivalence of trying to embody ethical witness within the deeply fallen world of national politics.

Fourth, shaped in part by his firm faith in the resurrection, Kiwanuka demonstrated great courage in the face of his own death, echoing the witness of the Uganda Martyrs of the 1880s. As early as the mid-1960s, he was privately reflecting on his own demise. "But as for myself I am going to leave my protection to God. If it pleases Him for me to die let it be. I shall do my work at His place. The only question is to be prepared at all times."[54] And as he wrote in his final letter to Amin on August 31, 1972, "For it is not death that I fear, for there is no one who has insurance against it . . . Let me hope, however, that the Almighty God will come in and vindicate the cause of the just."[55] It is not surprising that he refused his wife's and friends' pleas to flee Uganda, or Amin's entreaties that he sign a statement implicating Obote in his arrest. Kiwanuka died the way he lived—namely as an uncompromising "martyr" or "witness" to truth and justice. If politics seems so often based on a fear of death and a desire for false security, Kiwanuka offers an alternative Christian witness that "whoever wishes to save his life will lose it, but whoever loses his life for my sake and that of the gospel will save it" (Mark 8:35).

Finally, Kiwanuka embodies the promise of unfulfilled democratic politics in Uganda. His short stint in power and premature death robbed the country of one of its most promising civil leaders. As one Ugandan priest commented to me, "Kiwanuka was the one we missed. Our politics would be very different today if he had assumed power after independence."[56] In a country whose postcolonial history has been dominated by three seemingly "life presidents" backed by the military, Kiwanuka represents an alternative history. Would Ugandan politics have been demonstrably different if

53. Weber, "Politics as a Vocation," 23.

54. Kiwanuka, "Handwritten Note," 2.

55. Kiwanuka, Correspondence to Idi Amin Dada, August 31, 1972.

56. Author's field notes, September 2018.

Kiwanuka's DP had won the 1962 elections? Could he have controlled the military that dominates so much of postcolonial Ugandan life? Maybe so, maybe not. Regardless, Kiwanuka remains a symbol of what might have been. His beatification would be a symbol of Catholic hope that Uganda's political future might not mirror its bloody past.

Reflection Questions:

1. Which theological and political values should an ideal Christian or Catholic politician embody in your context?

2. The author implies that Kiwanuka's idealism undermined his political success. Is this a fair critique? Why or why not?

3. What do you see as the strengths and dangers of blending theological and political discourse?

4. Should Ben Kiwanuka be seen as a Catholic martyr? Should he be canonized as a saint? Why or why not?

2

The Bishop as Good Shepherd
Emmanuel Cardinal Nsubuga

TENS OF THOUSANDS OF Ugandans streamed into Nakivubo Stadium in Kampala on October 30, 1966. The fans gathered not to see the national soccer team but to witness the consecration of Emmanuel Kiwanuka Nsubuga as Uganda's second African Catholic archbishop. Fr. Clement Kiggundu's welcoming address captured the enthusiasm of the moment. "Half a million Catholics of his Archdiocese now have to look to him for instruction, advice and guidance . . . . People of other creeds will also look on him as a leader, not merely in spiritual and ecclesiastical matters, but also in other fields."[1] At the end of the Mass, Archbishop Nsubuga came forward to address the crowd. "It is true what the Pope's representative has said that I am your shepherd, your bishop. Do please heed to what I shall be telling you, knowing fully well that I shall be doing so in the name of the Lord. I am not for Catholics only; I am for you all."[2]

1. Mukasa et al., *Late Emmanuel Cardinal*, 3.
2. Kimbowa, *Emmanuel Cardinal Kiwanuka*, 57.

Figure 5

Over a subsequent quarter-century marred by dictatorship, war, and gross human rights violations, Nsubuga embodied his vow to be a shepherd for all of the Ugandan people. Nsubuga has not garnered the scholarly attention heaped on his trailblazing predecessor, Archbishop Joseph Kiwanuka, or his martyred Anglican contemporary, Archbishop Janani Luwum. But as the Archbishop of Kampala (1966–1990) and senior Catholic prelate during tumultuous years of political oppression and civil war, Nsubuga set a model for Uganda's postcolonial bishop. In essence, Nsubuga exercised a shepherd's ministry in social context. First, he embraced a preferential option for the poor and marginalized, reflecting the biblical shepherd's willingness to "leave the 99 in search of the one" (Matt 18:12). Second, he envisioned his ministry in terms of a broad ecumenical sheepfold, helping Uganda to move beyond a past marred by interreligious conflict and into a more collaborative interreligious future. Third, he exercised the shepherd's role of protecting and defending the sheep, utilizing both silence and prophetic speech to become one of the most important religious figures of political resistance in the early 1980s.[3] All of these commitments dovetail

3. To quote the Ugandan Muslim scholar A. B. K. Kasozi, "A number of Ugandans

with key dimensions of Catholic social teaching in the post-Vatican II era, including the option for the poor, reconciliation and ecumenism, and support for democracy. And as I will discuss at the end of the chapter, Nsubuga offers us important lessons for public religious leadership in terms of his prudential judgment, ecumenical bridge-building, and how he modeled pastoral authority with a common touch.

Highlighting a model bishop may seem obvious in a book on Catholic leadership in Uganda's public square. But bishops have not had much good press in recent years, especially in my own home country of the United States. The ongoing clergy sexual abuse scandal has revealed a toxic clericalist culture in which the hierarchy often seemed more concerned with damage-control than rooting out predatory child abusers. In politics, US bishops have been accused of being religious proxies for the Republican Party, reducing all of Catholic social teaching to the one nonnegotiable issue of opposing legal abortion. And even as they've become more vocal, the bishops' political voices seem increasingly irrelevant to the average American Catholic. Despite the elite Catholic angst that follows the quadrennial release of a USCCB "Faithful Citizenship" document, lay Catholics largely make their electoral decisions independent of the teachings of their church leaders.[4] Even Pope Francis has struggled to break through this impasse. Francis's efforts to advocate a consistent ethic of life—bringing together concern for the environment, the unborn, migrants, and the poor—shows little sign of cracking the "walls of separation" between America's entrenched ideological tribes of liberals and conservatives. In the face of such challenges, it can be easy to conclude that the Church's bishops should simply leave public life to public servants and go back to tending their flocks. After all, isn't it anachronistic to speak of a Catholic bishop's public leadership in ostensibly pluralistic and secular societies?

The tradition of Catholic social teaching, the teachings of Vatican II, and the social context of the Global South all push back on such a rhetorical

---

helped to bring out the truth. The most important was Emmanuel Cardinal Nsubuga, head of Uganda's Catholic church" (Kasozi, *Social Origins of Violence*, 162). The civil war was centered in the "Luweero Triangle" in south-central Uganda.

4. For example, a 2017 study by demographer William D'Antonio found that only 6 percent of Hillary Clinton voters and 10 percent of Donald Trump voters "try to follow the bishops' guidance and instructions" when it comes to voting. Over half of each group said they "consider the bishops' guidance but make up their own minds." Over one-third of each group agreed with the option that "bishops' views are irrelevant to my thinking on politics" (D'Antonio, "US Catholics," para. 15).

question. To be sure, modern politics and public life are primarily the arena of laity, as expressed in *Gaudium et Spes*, Vatican II's document on the Church in the Modern World. "It is to the laity, though not exclusively to them, that secular duties and activity properly belong."[5] But as evidenced by the "not exclusively" line, bishops retain a public role in the modern world, especially in terms of speaking on behalf of the poor and marginalized. In the words of the epochal 1968 Latin American Bishops (CELAM) conference at Medellín, Colombia, "The Latin American bishops cannot remain indifferent in the face of the tremendous social injustices existent in Latin America, which keep the majority of our peoples in dismal poverty."[6] Like their colleagues in Latin America, African bishops have been notable for their public activism on issues ranging from corruption and war to family planning and environmental degradation.

In reality, there is no faithful "withdrawal" option for the modern bishop; to say nothing gives a *carte blanche* to the powers-that-be. And while it's true that religious leaders inevitably have feet of clay (and sometimes worse), bishops have no monopoly on hypocrisy or sin, as anyone who has worked in politics, education, journalism, or the NGO world can attest. Modern Christian life also raises up profound examples of transformative episcopal leadership, from Joseph Cardinal Bernardin's seamless garment in Chicago to Archbishop Oscar Romero's defense of Salvadoran *campesinos* to Anglican Archbishop Desmond Tutu's Nobel Prize–winning efforts to bring down apartheid and build reconciliation in South Africa. Simply put, the question is not *whether* but *how* a bishop should engage public life. It is here that we can glean some important lessons from the life, witness, and teachings of Emmanuel Nsubuga.

The Life of Emmanuel Cardinal Nsubuga

Emmanuel Kiwanuka Nsubuga was born in November 1914 in Kisule Village, Singo County, Busuubizi Parish.[7] His home was located on the northern side of Buddu province, the Catholic bastion of the Buganda kingdom that was settled by Catholic chiefs after the Anglican-Catholic religious conflicts of the early 1890s (see the introduction). Nsubuga was one of

5. Second Vatican Council, *Gaudium et Spes,* sec. 43.

6. CELAM, "Document on the Poverty of the Church," 114.

7. Biographical information is drawn from Kimbowa, *Emmanuel Cardinal Kiwanuka,* 16–23, and Mukasa et al., *Late Emmanuel Cardinal,* 5–8.

eight children in a family known for its deep Marian piety. Like Benedicto Kiwanuka, Nsubuga also lived with relatives for much of his youth, spending years with his paternal aunt in Bukuumi, around seventy miles from his parental home. While attending primary school in Bukuumi, he encountered several of Buganda's first African priests. Inspired by their witness, Nsubuga entered Bukalasa Minor Seminary at the age of sixteen. Here he struggled with a series of health setbacks which delayed his progress. Despite concerns over his physical constitution, Nsubuga was promoted to Katigondo Major Seminary in 1937 and ordained a priest in December 1946 at the relatively advanced age of thirty-two.

Over the next fifteen years, Nsubuga made his mark in two separate Catholic parishes where he served as schools director, associate pastor, and pastor. He became known in the parishes for his motto of "let us pull up our socks and together we will succeed," a phrase he used to try to wean local Catholics from financial dependence on European missionaries and their wealthy home churches.[8] In June 1961, he was appointed as Vicar General of the Archdiocese of Rubaga (later renamed the Archdiocese of Kampala). As discussed previously, the Archbishop of Rubaga, Joseph Kiwanuka, was the first black Catholic bishop in modern sub-Saharan Africa and one of the most important Catholic leaders in colonial Africa. Before his episcopal appointment in 1939, Kiwanuka had also taught Nsubuga in the seminary. With Kiwanuka in Rome for the four sessions of Vatican II, Nsubuga served as the *de facto* diocesan coordinator during the early 1960s. The two men were very close, and it was Nsubuga who gave Kiwanuka last rites when the latter died on February 22, 1966. It did not come as a surprise, then, when in August 1966 the Holy See appointed Nsubuga as Archbishop of the newly created Archdiocese of Kampala. Reflecting his deep Marian devotion, Nsubuga adopted as his episcopal motto *Mater Profer Lumen Caecis*, or "Mary, Give Light to the Blind."[9]

Over the next quarter-century, Nsubuga's notable achievements included his invitation and hosting of the first papal visit to sub-Saharan Africa, a mission made famous by Pope Paul VI's 1969 call that "you Africans may, and must, have an African Christianity."[10] Nsubuga also oversaw the fundraising and construction of the Uganda Martyrs' Shrine at Namugongo on the northeastern side of Kampala. Finished in 1975, this shrine has

8. Kimbowa, *Emmanuel Cardinal Kiwanuka*, 33.

9. Kimbowa, *Emmanuel Cardinal Kiwanuka*, 35–59.

10. Orobator, *Theology Brewed*, 131.

become the premiere Catholic pilgrimage destination in Africa, drawing upwards of 2 to 3 million visitors for the annual June 3 feast of the Uganda Martyrs. In 1971, Nsubuga inaugurated St. Mbaaga's Seminary as a formation house for older men entering the seminary. At the height of Idi Amin's repression in 1976, Pope Paul VI endorsed his leadership by naming him as the first Cardinal in Ugandan history. Nsubuga went on to serve a very public role during the civil war of the early 1980s, as will be discussed later in this chapter. Shortly after his retirement in 1990, Nsubuga fell seriously ill. He died in April 1991 while seeking medical care in Germany. His body was flown back to Uganda and displayed at the parliamentary building before being moved to Rubaga Cathedral. For four days mourners filed past his body at Rubaga, reflecting the deep popular affection with which he was held.[11]

Taking on the Smell of the Sheep: Nsubuga's Preferential Option for the Poor

Since his election in March 2013, Pope Francis has insistently called on the Catholic Church to be a "poor church for the poor."[12] This call has challenged the Church to not only stand for the marginalized (e.g., the materially poor, refugees and immigrants, and the unborn) but to also embody a humbler, less grandiose institutional life. Francis has also called his bishops and priests to leave the sacristy and go into the streets, becoming shepherds who "take on the smell of the sheep."[13] The pope himself has matched his words with witness, whether in moving from the grand papal apartments to a nearby Vatican hotel or in welcoming Syrian refugees to live in Vatican City. Francis's mission reflects the broader call of Vatican II captured in the opening words of *Gaudium et Spes*: "The joy and hope, the grief and anguish of the men of our time, especially those who are poor or afflicted in any way, are the joy and hope, the grief and anguish of the followers of Christ as well."[14]

If one is looking for an African Catholic embodiment of this "poor church for the poor," Emmanuel Nsubuga could be a good model. In my interviews with survivors from the period, Nsubuga was repeatedly

11. Mugaaga, "Cardinal Nsubuga."

12. McElwee, "Pope Francis," para. 2.

13. Francis, *Evangelii Gaudium*, sec. 24.

14. Second Vatican Council, *Gaudium et Spes*, sec. 1.

remembered as humble and nonelitist, a pastor with a common touch who visited parishes, comforted refugees, hugged children, and loved the poor. In the words of his nephew, Fr. Henry Nsubuga Kiwanuka, "he hated to see people suffer . . . he was a lover of the poor, those who were helpless."[15] His Easter 1969 homily captures the ethos of Nsubuga's preferential option for the poor. "Hope, to be Christian, has to be effective for our fellow men. That means in a concrete way. Our hope has to give hope to them who are poor and 'left out' in our society, our hope has to kindle hope in them who have lost confidence in themselves and trust in the others."[16]

Nsubuga matched his words with pastoral actions. Like most Ugandan bishops, social development was a major preoccupation of his episcopate. His most important contribution in this regard was his initiation of Centennial Bank as the first Catholic-run banking network in Uganda; it is now the largest provider of microfinance in the country. He also started the Good Samaritan Sisters and the Amans Brothers, two religious congregations dedicated to working primarily among the poor, the disabled, and the destitute. Concerned with how large dowries were discouraging Catholic marriages, he offered to cover wedding expenses for poor Catholic couples who wished to marry in Rubaga Cathedral. Nsubuga also started Nalukolongo Home for the Disabled, Aged, and Destitute, a place where he volunteered every Friday. He loved Nalukolongo so much that he requested to be buried there rather than the bishops' traditional resting place at Rubaga Cathedral. In the words of former Nalukolongo administrator Sr. Theresa Basemera, "he thought that if he was buried here, people will not forget the poor."[17] His small shrine at Nalukolongo remains a popular spot for prayer in Kampala.

Nsubuga thus stands as an important witness of "the poor church for the poor," especially for an African hierarchy and clergy that has struggled at times to embody simplicity. Far from closeting himself away from the poor, he opened his life and his church to them.

Broadening the Sheepfold: Nsubuga's Ecumenical Mission

Since Vatican II, the Catholic Church has also embraced ecumenism and interreligious dialogue as constituent parts of its mission. In his address

15. Henry Nsubuga Kiwanuka, interview.

16. Nsubuga, "Easter Message 1969," 2.

17. Basemera, interview, June 30, 2015.

opening the council in October 1962, Pope John XXIII stated "the unity of mankind" as one of Vatican II's primary goals.[18] *Unitatis Redintegratio*, Vatican II's decree on Christian ecumenism, built on this mandate by positing that "the restoration of unity among all Christians is one of the principal concerns of the Second Vatican Council."[19] The 1965 document *Nostra Aetate* extended this mission further into relations between Catholics and non-Christians: "the Church, therefore, exhorts her sons, that through dialogue and collaboration with the followers of other religions, carried out with prudence and love and in witness to the Christian faith and life, they recognize, preserve and promote the good things, spiritual and moral, as well as the socio-cultural values found among these men."[20] As with the option for the poor, this ecumenical and interreligious commitment has been embraced by all post-Vatican II popes up to and including Pope Francis. Here, too, Nsubuga also made a major mark in Uganda, reflecting his promise on his consecration day to be a "shepherd for you all."

First, Nsubuga continued and expanded on his predecessor Archbishop Joseph Kiwanuka's legacy as a committed Christian ecumenist. Kiwanuka had collaborated with his Anglican counterpart, Archbishop Leslie Brown, to start the Uganda Joint Christian Council (UJCC) in 1964. After 1966, Emmanuel Nsubuga served in the leadership of the UJCC, and he initiated a new UJCC Committee for Ecumenism in 1969. Later that year, he exchanged a ritual kiss of peace with his close friend and fellow *muganda* bishop, the Anglican Dunstan Nsubuga. In the early 1980s, he hosted the first-ever visit of the Anglican Archbishop of Canterbury to Rubaga Cathedral.[21] His religious outreach also extended to Islam. In 1967, he became the first Ugandan Catholic leader to pay a formal visit to a Muslim community, and he later supported the construction of a mosque and a Catholic church on the site where Muslims had hosted the first White Father missionaries in 1879.[22] For Nsubuga, ecumenical collaboration necessitated a "change of heart" on the part of both Catholics and Protestants, recapturing the spirit of ecumenical solidarity that marked the witness of the original Uganda Martyrs.[23] As he wrote in one Lent 1973 pastoral letter, "Do not let

18. John XXIII, "Pope John's Opening Speech," para. 37.

19. Second Vatican Council, *Unitatis Redintegratio*, sec. 1.

20. Second Vatican Council, *Nostra Aetate*, sec. 2.

21. Mukasa, *Late Emmanuel Cardinal*, 14.

22. Kimbowa, *Emmanuel Cardinal Kiwanuka*, 181.

23. Nsubuga, "Address to Makerere Students."

the differences in our religions divide us because there is no religion that teaches people to hate those of a different religion. Every religion teaches us to LOVE ONE ANOTHER."[24]

Critically, though, Nsubuga also recognized how the ecumenical movement could establish the churches as united bulwarks during bouts of severe political repression. For example, between 1973 and 1975, Nsubuga worked with Anglican leaders to raise concerns with General Idi Amin Dada, Uganda's self-declared "Life President" who had taken power in a military coup in January 1971 (see introduction).[25] Writing on behalf of the UJCC in May 1975, Nsubuga and Anglican Archbishop Luwum expressed their "anxieties and grave concerns" over Uganda's growing abrogation of human rights and the severe punishments meted out for criminal infractions, such as instituting the death penalty for smuggling.[26] In August 1976, Nsubuga and Luwum called together Anglican, Catholic, and Muslim leaders for an off-the-record meeting to discuss the state of the nation. Although no public statements emerged from this gathering, the assembled leaders lamented the growing killings, looting, and abuses of Amin's dreaded State Research Bureau and the Public Security Unit. Leaked minutes from this meeting reached Amin's desk.[27] Inflamed at this growing ecumenical opposition, Amin took Archbishop Luwum's and Cardinal Nsubuga's Christmas 1976 sermons off the radio and threatened Christian leaders who "preach bloodshed rather than peace."[28] In the case of Luwum, Amin followed through on his threats, personally assassinating him at the Intercontinental Conference Center in Kampala on February 16, 1977.[29] For his part, Nsubuga lived under virtual house arrest through the remaining years of the Amin regime. Close confidants speculate that Nsubuga only survived because of Amin's fears of the Vatican and international reaction.[30]

In summary, the "Cardinal of Uganda" embodied his 1966 promise at his consecration that as a religious shepherd, he was "not just for the

24. Nsubuga, "*Obudde Obw'ekisiibo*," sec. 41 (emphases in text). I thank George Mpanga for his translations from Cardinal Nsubuga's Luganda-language letters.

25. Dunstan Nsubuga, quoted in "UJCC Agenda, 9 November 1973."

26. Luwum and Nsubuga, "UJCC Memorandum."

27. Ford, *Janani*, 74; Kivengere, *I Love Idi Amin*, 42.

28. See here the December 27, 1976 issue of *Uganda Empya*.

29. Luwum remains one of the most prominent twentieth-century martyrs for the Church of Uganda and the worldwide Anglican Communion. On Luwum's death and legacy, see Ward, "Archbishop Janani Luwum," 199–224.

30. Ssenngendo, interview.

Catholics—I am for you all."[31] In this regard, he recognized that standing for the common good entails a bishop standing not just with Catholics, but with the entire community. This in turn reflects the broad social and communal leadership roles played by bishops in Uganda and throughout Africa. In other words, African bishops are not only seen as denominational leaders of the Catholic sheepfold, but also as esteemed elders and civil society leaders.[32] Nsubuga's outreach was especially significant in Uganda, given the bitter denominational competition and historical rivalry between Anglican and Catholic factions in Uganda. Ugandan religious leaders have continued this spirit of collaboration on behalf of the common good, whether in the Acholi Religious Leaders Peace Initiative (ARLPI) in northern Uganda or more recent efforts to kickstart a "national dialogue" for Uganda.[33]

Protecting the Sheepfold: Nsubuga's Resistance to Dictatorship

This leads us to Nsubuga's third embodiment of the bishop as public shepherd—namely through a politics of nonviolent resistance toward those who would attack the sheep. Here Nsubuga stands in line with other post-Vatican II Catholic bishops who helped lead popular resistance to authoritarian governments, including Archbishop Oscar Romero in El Salvador, Cardinal Jaime Sin and the "Rosary Revolution" in 1980s Philippines, and Pope John Paul II and the Solidarity movement in communist Poland.

Like Romero early in his episcopal career, Emmanuel Nsubuga was not initially viewed as a prophet for social justice and political resistance. In fact, for years after his promotion to the episcopate in 1966, he shied away from formal public comments on political matters. For example, in his Christmas 1966 message, Nsubuga made no mention of Obote's ongoing state of emergency in Buganda, the expanded detention of political opponents, or Obote's proposed constitutional revision.[34] His 1967 independence anniversary letter, entitled "For God and My Country," also remained on the

31. In the words of George Mpanga, my Anglican research assistant, "We grew up calling him the Cardinal of Uganda."

32. This phenomenon is even more evident in Uganda's neighbor, the Democratic Republic of the Congo. See Carney, "Bishop is Governor Here," 97–122.

33. I talk more about the Acholi Religious Leaders' Peace Initiative in chapter 6. On the latter effort, see Murungi, "National Dialogue."

34. Nsubuga, "Christmas Message."

level of platitudes, exhorting Ugandan citizens to "abide to the Principles of Religion, and do all things for the Good of the Country."[35] He issued no response to Obote's 1969 Common Man's Charter or the 1970 Nakivubo Pronouncements, economic directives that embodied Obote's "Move to the Left" toward a more state-led, socialist economy. As mentioned previously, Nsubuga collaborated with Archbishop Luwum to lobby Idi Amin, but he never wrote in an official capacity on Amin's brutal abrogation of human rights, in contrast to Luwum's and the Anglicans' more forceful statements.[36] Nor did his fellow Catholic bishops; the Ugandan Episcopal Conference did not issue any joint pastoral letters between 1963 and 1979. Defenders point out that Nsubuga was "more of a speaker than a writer" and that he tried to "expose the truth without attacking the government."[37] But compared to a figure like Luwum, Nsubuga could be justly critiqued for his failure to exercise a more prophetic voice during the 1960s and 1970s, contributing to an era described even by Ugandan Catholic scholars as a "period of great silence."[38]

It was in the post-1979 context of unsettled politics and civil war that Nsubuga found his public voice of resistance. First, Nsubuga collaborated with representatives of the Muslim, Anglican, and Orthodox traditions to condemn Uganda's worsening climate of political insecurity and violence. Writing in July 1979, these religious leaders lambasted the "soul-searing insecurity" that had marked the Amin years: "People were kidnapped, murdered in cold blood, robbed of their property and denied their human rights."[39] They also lobbied President Milton Obote's government behind the scenes. In a September 1981 meeting with Obote, Nsubuga and several

35. Nsubuga, "For God," 1.

36. In a February 1977 letter to Amin, Luwum and the Anglican bishops issued their most forceful denunciation of the regime. "'The gun whose muzzle has been pressed against the Archbishop's stomach, the gun which has been used to search the Bishop of Bukedi's houses, is a gun which is being pointed at every Christian in the Church. We have buried many who have died as a result of being shot and there are many more whose bodies have not been found, yet their disappearance is connected with the activities of some members of the Security Forces" (Muhima, "Fellowship of His Suffering," 144–45).

37. Wamala, interview; Kimbowa, interview.

38. Ssettuuma et al., "Social Teaching," 21–22. In their words, "the great silence in terms of the church's social teaching during this time reflects the social history of repression, and the gradual naturalization of violence and a culture of survival" (21). Others have attributed the lack of pastoral letters to ethnic divisions within the episcopal conference (Author's field notes, June 2015).

39. "Four Religious Leaders."

other religious leaders lamented that the "lack of [army] discipline has caused rampant torture, robbery, killing and raping," described Uganda as "bleeding to death," and named specific abuses in ten different communities.[40] The specificity here is notable given the often-platitudinous nature of church statements on politics.

Second, Nsubuga worked together with his fellow Catholic bishops to speak out boldly on Uganda's political violence, effectively ending the "period of great silence." This is especially evident in the Ugandan Episcopal Conference's 1980 pastoral letter, "I Have Heard the Cry of My People." Echoing YHWH's compassion for his enslaved people in their "hour of great sorrow" in Exodus 1–3, Nsubuga and the UEC described themselves as "your shepherds, close to you with sympathy, fatherly love and solidarity," and promised to be a "voice of the poor and of the oppressed, the defenders of truth and right, the agents of reconciliation and conversion."[41] Similarly, in a subsequent pastoral letter in 1982, the Catholic bishops lambasted the "way of death" that embodied Uganda's political situation. "Mutual fear becomes the rule, competition becomes callous and deceitful, violence is exercised with weapons of death, and the entire system of justice is set aside to make way for a system of spies, torture and illegal executions."[42] In his own personal statements, Nsubuga also called out the perpetrators of political violence. For example, he dedicated his All Souls' Day 1980 message to all victims of violence in Uganda, calling on Catholics to

> pray for the nameless victims whose bodies are left on our city sidewalks, in ditches and garbage dumps . . . Let us pray for the MURDERERS who are all around us, those who pull the trigger, those who provide weapons, those who hire the killers, and those who praise them . . . and those who cast a cover of silence over individual killings and over mass murder, thus approving by their murderous silence the existing violence.[43]

In an Advent 1981 pastoral letter, he exhorted Uganda's political leaders to "remember that you vowed to protect people, but not to persecute them unjustly,"[44] grounding his prophetic critiques in CST's fundamental principle of human dignity. "If we fail to know that a fellow human being

40. Ugandan Religious Leaders, "In Search for Peace," 1.

41. Ugandan Episcopal Conference, "I Have Heard," sec. 3.

42. Ugandan Episcopal Conference, "In God We Trust," sec. 6.

43. Nsubuga, "Message of His Eminence," 12–13 (emphases original).

44. Nsubuga, *Obudde Bw'Amatuuka*, 8.

has dignity that comes from God, a dignity that no one should take away from him, and no one can replace, if we fail to know that I have concern for a fellow human, we cannot count ourselves the good people of God."[45]

Nsubuga also matched his prophetic words with pastoral care. Throughout the early 1980s, he negotiated the release of political prisoners, provided support for relatives of the disappeared, and brought supplies to war zones. He once flew a papal flag on his car to facilitate the movement of a caravan of Red Cross trucks carrying refugees on the two-hour journey from Mityana to Kampala.[46] In 1981 and 1982, he opened Rubaga Cathedral to more than 1,000 internally displaced people. Suspecting NRA guerrillas were mixing among the civilians, UNLF soldiers accosted parishioners during Ash Wednesday Mass in February 1982 and ransacked Nsubuga's personal residence. Several days later, Nsubuga called a packed press conference to publicly denounce the Obote regime's transgression of the principle of sanctuary, precipitating a formal government apology.[47]

In 1985, Nsubuga assumed the role of public diplomat. After four years of brutal fighting, the tide of war had turned against Obote's government. Toppled in another military coup, Obote fled the country in July, paving the way for a fresh round of negotiations between General Tito Okello's Uganda National Liberation Army (UNLA) and Museveni's NRA. Reflecting his moral stature inside Uganda and likely back-channel dialogues with the NRA, Nsubuga was called on to help mediate Nairobi peace talks between the two sides.[48] Sensing he could win a military victory, Museveni resisted making concessions, and the talks stalled around Christmas. On January 21, 1986, Nsubuga called a press conference in which he made an impassioned appeal for peace, couching this in terms of Uganda's national motto. "Let me reiterate the outcry of the sons and daughters of Uganda: children, widows, orphans, displaced people and everybody are appealing to all the fighting groups to stop shedding blood. I say all this FOR GOD AND MY COUNTRY."[49] On January 26, Museveni's NRM took Kampala and brought

45. Nsubuga, *Obudde Bw'Amatuuka*, 5.

46. Kimbowa, *Emmanuel Cardinal Kiwanuka*, 158.

47. Nsubuga, "Press Statement." Although government forces found no arms in Nsubuga's residence or the cathedral, rumors persist that he was a clandestine sympathizer of the NRM who sent emissaries to make contact with Museveni in the early 1980s (Author's field notes, June 2015, July 2017, February 2019).

48. Nsubuga, "Correspondence to General Tito Okello"; Nsubuga, "Points to be Discussed."

49. Nsubuga, "Press Conference," 5 (emphases original).

the war to an end in southern Uganda. Five months later, Cardinal Nsubuga and the Catholic bishops called for a "fundamental change" in the nature of Ugandan politics, exhorting Uganda's new leaders to base their politics on human dignity, social justice, the common good, and reconciliation.[50]

Cardinal Nsubuga's Leadership Legacies

In summary, Cardinal Nsubuga embraced key post-Vatican II Catholic priorities in the public sphere concerning the preferential option for the poor, ecumenism, and resistance to dictatorship. He will also be remembered for his construction of new seminaries, establishment of new religious communities, and, perhaps most of all, his inauguration of the Uganda Martyrs Shrine at Namugongo. In closing, I would highlight three key leadership lessons that emerge from his social witness as a bishop.

First and foremost, he embodied the role of a "shepherd for all." One of Nsubuga's oft-repeated lines was his joke that "I have no certificate but my baptismal certificate."[51] On one level, this line undergirded Nsubuga's lack of pretension. If Joseph Kiwanuka is remembered for his intellectual brilliance, Emmanuel Nsubuga is remembered for his common touch, such as his willingness to lift up children in the air or his penchant for pastoral aphorisms, such as comparing the uprooting of sin to a tractor clearing the bush in a field.[52] More substantively, however, this line pointed to Nsubuga's grounding of his Christian identity in baptism, a sacrament he saw as enabling Christians to become seeds of unity and peace in the "tribe of God" (*ggwanga lya Katonda*).[53] His emphasis on this shared Christian identity helped defuse the Anglican-Catholic rivalry and religio-political tribalism that marked so much of Ugandan colonial history. As discussed previously, his ecumenical relationships also helped church leaders to present a more united opposition to Amin's and Obote's repressive regimes in the 1970s and 1980s. For Nsubuga, this public witness reflected not the politicization of the church, but rather the church's obligation to stand in solidarity with and to protect the common people. In his words, "as a Religious Leader,

50. Uganda Episcopal Conference, "With a New Heart," secs. 9, 21, 44.

51. Kimbowa, *Emmanuel Cardinal Kiwanuka*, 48.

52. Nsubuga, "Tweyambise Obudde," sec. 2. The former story was shared by George Mpanga, recalling Cardinal Nsubuga's lifting him in the air during a visit to his home village in the 1980s (Author's field notes, June 2015 and June 2019).

53. Nsubuga, *"Okukuza Ekyasa,"* sec. 8.

it is not my task to run the politics of Uganda, but as a shepherd it is my obligation to work for peace among the people of God."[54] This public stance did not equal strict political neutrality, and critics have accused him—with some merit—of being first a DP supporter and later an NRM advocate.[55] But in part due to his age as well as the Church's access to international resources, Nsubuga remained a shepherd rather than a sheep; he worked with political authorities but did not become their client. For example, despite his close working relationship with Museveni, who made a habit of consulting with the Cardinal at his farm in the late 1980s, Nsubuga still spoke out against NRA atrocities in Kumi district in eastern Uganda in July 1989. Important here was Nsubuga's willingness to name rather than hide the relationship, and his recognition that personal relationship should not compromise his greater responsibility to the common good. "By giving me heads of cattle Museveni has not shut up my mouth at all. I shall speak out whenever he is going astray."[56]

Second, Nsubuga offered a leadership style defined by the virtue of prudence. One can justifiably criticize Nsubuga for his failure to speak out more forcefully as the shadows of political oppression grew darker during the 1960s and early 1970s. Although his homilies were recalled as politically pointed, he wrote no public letter critiquing Amin's government.[57] On the other hand, publicly condemning Amin would likely have led to his death, following in the footsteps of Benedicto Kiwanuka or Janani Luwum. There is clearly a central place for the martyrs in the Christian tradition. As Michael Budde has argued, martyrs embody the church's witness as "the new people formed by God as disciples of Christ, whose murdered and resurrected body is the paradigmatic witness to God's love of and hope for the world."[58] But their heroic example unto death can also be exaggerated to the exclusion of other forms of faithful public witness (the hyperbole is even

54. Nsubuga, "Statement by H. E. Emmanuel Cardinal K. Nsubuga."

55. For example, Milton Obote's biographer, Kenneth Ingham, describes Nsubuga as "at one with the Democratic Party," attributing political tensions in the 1980s in part to Roman Catholic leaders' determination to hold out for a DP victory (Ingham, *Obote*, 206). Through the 1980s, Ugandan Catholics were assumed to be DP members or supporters; this association has faded under NRM rule.

56. Kimbowa, *Emmanuel Cardinal Kiwanuka*, 162. The age differential helped here. Nsubuga was in his seventies at this point, whereas Museveni was only in his forties.

57. Author's field notes, June 2015. Unfortunately, I have not been able to obtain written copies of Cardinal Nsubuga's sermons from the 1970s.

58. Budde and Scott, *Witness of the Body*, viii.

more frustrating when propagated by first-world academics living safe and comfortable lives in their university offices). Not only can a desire for martyrdom get intertwined with spiritual pride, as was arguably the case with Archbishop Luwum or Ben Kiwanuka,[59] but living to see another day can benefit the long-term community. In turn, Nsubuga's silence should not be seen as signaling his support for the regime. He was never accused of being a secret supporter of Amin, much less Obote. Rather, he kept silent, neither endorsing nor lambasting the regime. In this sense, Nsubuga reminds us that there are alternative Christian leadership approaches between the opposing poles of "martyr" and "collaborator." He also reminds us of the need for prudential judgment; sometimes one is called to speak out, but sometimes it is better to keep quiet. One should not fear martyrdom, but to echo Thomas More, one should also not seek to be a martyr.

Third, Nsubuga's witness reminds us of the importance of genuine spiritual authority. Americans live in modern Western cultures highly suspicious of authority, whether political, religious, cultural, or intellectual; elites of all stripes are so often the targets of righteous indignation and angry *ressentiment*.[60] Yet even if the institutional Catholic triumphalism of the pre-Vatican II era is best left to the dustbin of history, genuine pastoral authority is necessary in any era, carrying forward Jesus's own model of *exousia*, in which power serves the cause of freedom.[61] In this regard, Cardinal Nsubuga stands out, continually remembered for having "no fear" of political governments.[62] In the words of one local lay leader who survived the Amin-Obote period, "The Catholic Church had pride at that time. They [the government] feared them. If you touched the bishop you were touching the Holy See—that's Rome!"[63] In a hierarchical ecclesial and social culture like that found in Uganda, any Catholic archbishop will receive a certain

---

59. Archbishop Luwum's wife and colleagues begged him to leave the country in the days leading up to his 1977 assassination. In dismissing his wife's pleas, Luwum utilized soteriological language to describe his potential sacrifice. "I will go [to meet the President]. Even if he kills me, my blood will save the nation" (Ford, *Janani*, 84–85). Benedicto Kiwanuka expressed similar sentiments in the days leading up to his own death, as discussed in chapter 1.

60. See Mishra, *Age of Anger*.

61. Kittel and Friedrich, *Theological Dictionary of the New Testament*, 238–39.

62. When asked to describe Nsubuga, multiple priests from the era highlighted his courage and lack of fear toward the ruling authorities of his day (Kalyabbe, interview; Kanyerezi, interview; Gavamukulya, interview; Magunda, interview).

63. Mpiima, interview.

modicum of respect. But Nsubuga's humility and joy in meeting people in their lives also earned popular affection and goodwill. In summary, Nsubuga embodied two of the most common phrases attributed to Jesus Christ in the Gospels: "He spoke with authority, not as their scribes," and "Be not afraid."[64] In this regard, he is a "good shepherd" worthy of emulation.

Reflection Questions

1. The author highlights the image of "shepherd" for the bishop. What other biblical or cultural images would you apply to a bishop?

2. Should Cardinal Nsubuga have spoken out more forcefully against Amin in the 1970s? Did he become "too political" in the 1980s? Why or why not?

3. If a local Catholic bishop called you into his office to discuss how he should respond to the social challenges facing your community, what advice would you give him?

64. Examples of the first passage would include Mark 1:22 and Matthew 7:29. Derivatives of "Be Not Afraid" are found in over twenty places in the gospels alone, including Matthew 14:27, Luke 5:10, and Mark 5:36.

3

Uganda's Liberation Theologian

Fr. John Mary Waliggo

IT WAS A HOT day in January 1983. Government agents turned rooms upside down, scouring a remote home in southern Uganda for a priest who had been described as the most dangerous man in Uganda. Banging loudly on the door, they entered a bedroom only to find a scared adolescent girl cowering on a bed.

"Where is Father Waliggo?" they barked.

The girl refused to speak. The soldiers ordered the girl to arise so that they could search under her bed. She demurred. They demanded that she leave the room. She stayed still. As one exasperated soldier laid an arm on the girl to forcibly remove her, he noticed blood on the sheets.

"It is my time of the month," the girl murmured.

Sensing the transgression of a taboo, the soldiers turned and left the room. Minutes later, Fr. John Mary Waliggo emerged from under the bed. That night, the girl's family and friends dressed him as a Catholic nun and drove him to the border town of Kabale. Under cover of darkness, he slipped across the Rwanda border and into exile.[1]

If this anecdote sounds more like Jason Bourne than Fulton Sheen, you are not alone in thinking this. But such was the remarkable life of Fr. John Mary Waliggo, Uganda's foremost Catholic intellectual in the latter half of the twentieth century. As a church historian and theologian, Waliggo made an indelible impact on scholarship concerning the Ugandan Catholic

---

1. Ssettuuma, interview, June 26, 2015.

58

Church. As a political activist, secretary of the 1995 constitutional commission, and commissioner for Uganda's National Human Rights Commission, Waliggo played critical roles in the early years of Yoweri Museveni's National Resistance Movement government. And if there was one current that ran through his life as well as his scholarship, it was the theopolitical concept of "liberation."

To contextualize Waliggo, a little background on the broader movement of liberation theology is necessary. The most important public or political theology of the late twentieth century, liberation theology originated through the work of scholars, bishops, and local Christian communities in Latin America.[2] I will summarize its teachings in four movements. First, theology was understood as critical reflection on Christian praxis in light of the word of God. In other words, God's revelation should be read in light of one's own particular historical, cultural, and social context, and reflection should always be accompanied by action. Second, within a Latin American social context of deep political and economic inequality and social stratification, salvation could be best described in the language of "liberation." This would include liberation from the bondage of both personal and structural sin, liberation from economic exploitation, and liberation from the type of fatalism that allowed the poor to accept their poverty as "God's will." Toward this end, the Bible should be read through a "liberating hermeneutic," an interpretive lens highlighting God's work for freedom in Exodus and the prophetic literature as well as Jesus's proclamation of the Reign of God.[3] Third, liberation theologians looked to break the institutional Church's longtime alliance with the wealthy, calling on the Church to take the side of the poor masses through encouraging structural social change via land reform, community action, and agricultural cooperatives. In this regard, liberation theologians argued that the fundamental religious

2. At a scholarly level, the movement is often traced to a 1964 gathering of theologians at Petropolis, Brazil, although the first breakthrough theological work came seven years later in Gustavo Gutièrrez's *Theology of Liberation*. At the popular level, thousands of Base Christian Communities made up of lay Catholic families were encouraged to read the Scriptures in light of their own social context. The pedagogical approach here borrowed from the Brazilian education theorist Paolo Freire's notion of "education for freedom," namely using education to raise the poor's consciousness of their own deprivation and how to remedy it. On the history of liberation theology in Latin America, see Tombs, *Latin American Liberation*.

3. See, for example, Luke 4:18: "The Spirit of the Lord is upon me, because he has anointed me to bring glad tidings to the poor. He has sent me to proclaim liberty to captives and recovery of sight to the blind, to let the oppressed go free."

challenge in Latin America was "not the nonbeliever, but the nonperson: the millions who were deprived of basic physical necessities and elementary human rights."[4] Fourth, the movement was endorsed and pastorally implemented by the Church's leadership at the second and third general conferences of the Latin American Bishops at Medellín, Colombia, in 1968, and at Puebla, Mexico, in 1979. In the words of Medellín,

> the Latin American bishops cannot remain indifferent in the face of the tremendous social injustices existent in Latin America, which keep the majority of our peoples in dismal poverty, which in many cases becomes inhuman wretchedness. A deafening cry pours from the throats of millions of men and women asking their pastors for a liberation that reaches them from nowhere else.[5]

The Latin American bishops in turn reflected and influenced the Roman magisterium's deeper turn toward the social question in the 1960s and 1970s, especially through the writings of Pope John XXIII, Vatican II, and Pope Paul VI on poverty, peace, and development.[6]

In contrast to Latin America, liberation theology had a more muted impact in Africa. To be sure, the related movement of "Black Theology" emerged in 1970s South Africa's context of racial apartheid and white authoritarianism, a setting in which Bishop Desmond Tutu described theology as "a cry from the crucible of human suffering and anguish which asserted the fundamental humanity of the victim."[7] Likewise, the Cameroonian Jesuit Jean-Marc Éla was an important progenitor of liberation theology in West Africa in the 1980s, arguing that theology's pressing task was to rehabilitate the "marginalized masses" and liberate a "dependent church among oppressed peoples."[8] But in general, postcolonial African theology was more preoccupied with questions of inculturation—namely how to retrieve the insights of traditional African culture after a century of European

4. Tombs, *Latin American Liberation*, 191.

5. CELAM, "Document on the Poverty," 114.

6. I would highlight here John XXIII's social teachings in *Mater et Magistra* (1961) and *Pacem en Terris* (1963), Vatican II's constitution on the church and the modern world, *Gaudium et Spes* (1965), Pope Paul VI's encyclical on development, *Populorum Progressio* (1967), and the Catholic bishops' special synod on "Justice in the World" (1971).

7. Tutu, "Theology of Liberation in Africa," 163.

8. Éla, *African Cry*, 6, 38. Other key early works of African liberation theology include Buthelezi, "African Theology?"; Boesak, *Farewell to Innocence*; Biko, *Black Consciousness in South Africa*; Eboussi-Boulaga, *Christianity without Fetishes*; Mosala, *Biblical Hermeneutics and Black Theology*.

colonial repression—than with questions of sociopolitical liberation.[9] And although African bishops and missionaries shared the Latin American emphasis on base communities, the African model of "Small Christian Communities" tended to be much more devotional and apolitical than their Latin American counterparts.[10]

Waliggo challenged this separation of theology, inculturation, and politics in Uganda. Although his is not an international household name like Desmond Tutu, Waliggo, like Tutu, had a huge impact in his own country through his writings, his pastoral work, and his extensive contributions to constitutionalism and human rights. A teacher, writer, and civil servant, Waliggo embodies the role of the "priest in public," and his extensive corpus of theological work testifies to the potential power of an African theology of liberation.

9. As we will see, Waliggo argued that inculturation and liberation should go hand in hand. On African inculturation theology, see Nyamiti, *Christ as Our Ancestor*; Bujo, *African Christian Morality*; Bediako, *Christianity in Africa*; Magesa, *Anatomy of Inculturation*; Magesa, *What is Not Sacred?*

10. See Healey, "Basic Christian Communities"; Carney, "People Bonded Together by Love."

"There are people that when you speak of them, you almost want to take off your hat":[11] The Life of Fr. John Mary Waliggo

FIGURE 6

John Mary Waliggo was born in 1942 in Bisanje, a small village in Buddu province, the traditional Catholic bastion of Buganda kingdom.[12] As discussed in the introduction, Buddu had been settled by thousands of exiled Catholics in the aftermath of the 1888–1892 "religious wars." Waliggo's extended family included Muslims, Traditionalists, Anglicans, and Catholics, shaping his ecumenical sensibilities from a young age. His uncle, Fr. Timeo Ssemogerere, was, along with future bishop Joseph Kiwanuka, the first Ugandan to earn a doctorate in canon law in Rome in the 1930s.[13] His mother, father, and maternal grandmother were all devout Catholics. His grandmother was an especially important influence. The daughter of a Toro chief, she was briefly enslaved during the revolutions of the 1890s. Freed in part due to the intervention of White Father missionaries, Waliggo's

11. Wasswa Mpagi, interview.

12. This biographical sketch draws from Ssettuuma, interview, July 6, 2017; Ssettuuma, *Thief on the Plane*. The latter includes many of Waliggo's first-person reflections on his life.

13. Nanseera, interview.

grandmother later served as a cook in the local minor seminary at Bukalasa where she saw her work as raising up "priests who will fight slavery."[14]
Her lifelong association of Catholicism with resistance and liberation was
very influential in Waliggo's own development, as was his conviction that
his mother had been unjustly denied professional opportunities due to her
gender.[15]

Growing up around Bukalasa, Waliggo was drawn to the priesthood,
and he entered the minor seminary at age eleven in 1953. His family lacked
money for school fees, and Waliggo worried constantly that he would be
expelled. For this reason, he used to hide behind a larger student every
time the administrator showed up to collect school fees. This priest finally
called him out one day. "John, study in freedom! Don't be afraid. Don't hide
yourself!"[16] The priest took a liking to Waliggo and ensured he could stay
in seminary at a reduced rate. More importantly, the association of freedom
with the casting out of fear became a lifelong mantra for Waliggo.

In seminary, Waliggo proved to be a brilliant student who demonstrated an early talent to systematize and simplify. As one former classmate recalls, "If we failed to understand a lecturer, we would consult John
Waliggo!"[17] He also had an independent streak and regularly crossed hairs
with some of the more traditionalist professors; such internal ecclesial resistance would remain a theme throughout his life. Waliggo did have his
champions, though, including Adrian Hastings, the great Catholic historian
of Africa who came to Bukalasa seminary in 1959 to serve as a missionary
and teacher. Hastings became a lifelong mentor to Waliggo, shaping the
young seminarian's interests in the intersections of theology and history,
church and state, and "liberation based on critical social analysis."[18]

In 1966, Bishop Adrian Ddungu sent Waliggo to study theology at
Urbaniana, the pontifical university in Rome dedicated to mission and the
global church. He served as president of the international seminarians' association and organized seminars on African theology that drew the likes
of Karl Rahner and Jean Danielou. Conversations with Latin American
seminarians helped him recognize some of the shared structural and social
challenges of Third World countries. Always pushing the boundaries, he

14. Ssettuuma, interview, July 6, 2017.

15. Bugembe, interview.

16. Ssettuuma, interview, July 6, 2017.

17. Kasule, interview.

18. Ssettuuma, *Thief on the Plane*, 27.

conducted research on the Roman church's "apostolate to prostitutes," a project he later claimed "nearly cost me my vocation" due to the behavior he uncovered among high-ranking prelates in Rome.[19] Such ecclesial hypocrisy gave him pause on whether he should go through with ordination. His spiritual advisor, future Cardinal Emmanuel Wamala, helped place his priestly vocation in christological perspective, a perspective that ultimately sustained Waliggo's vocation: "We are for the Church, but there are so many weaknesses in the Church. We are for Christ above all."[20]

After his ordination in 1970, Waliggo enrolled in the doctoral program in history at the University of Cambridge. Working under Prof. John Iliffe, Waliggo conducted groundbreaking ethnographic history on Catholic history in Buganda province between 1880 and 1925. Defended in 1976, his dissertation remains the preeminent scholarly analysis of early Catholic missions in Buganda.[21] His studies at Cambridge also facilitated travels to West Africa, South America, and the United States, where he researched the Atlantic slave trade and America's legal discrimination against African Americans and Chinese immigrants in the late nineteenth century. Waliggo even had the opportunity to preach at Martin Luther King's home church, Ebenezer Baptist, in Atlanta.

As early as his seminarian days in the 1960s, Waliggo wrote on political controversies in Uganda, assuming a pseudonym as he critiqued Milton Obote's government for its growing authoritarianism.[22] His political critiques grew more pronounced after Amin came to power in the 1970s. After defending his dissertation at Cambridge and spending six months researching in the White Fathers archives in Rome, Waliggo took the risk of sneaking back into Uganda. He later wrote that returning to Uganda in 1977 "made me turn from history to human rights activist . . . I decided to fully utilize my theology and study of history to fight for justice and peace, democracy and human rights in Uganda."[23] Amin's agents quickly began tracking Waliggo, and in September 1977 he fled to the Ssese Islands in Lake Victoria. Ever the scholar, he used this six-month exile period to conduct

19. Waliggo, quoted in Ssettuuma, *Thief on the Plane*, 34.

20. Nanseera, interview.

21. Waliggo, "Catholic Church in the Buddu Province."

22. Unfortunately, these early writings have been lost (Ssettuuma, interview, July 6, 2017).

23. Ssettuuma, *Thief on the Plane*, 48. Waliggo's later scholarship also mirrored this trajectory from history to sociopolitical activism. See Waliggo, "Catholic Church and the Root-Cause"; Waliggo, "Role of Christian Churches."

ethnographic research on traditional religious practice on all sixty-four of the populated islands. He returned to mainland Uganda in 1978, keeping a very low profile in a rural parish in Rakai in the Diocese of Masaka.

Waliggo embraced the relative political opening that followed the toppling of Amin's government in April 1979. In the run-up to Uganda's first democratic elections in nearly two decades in December 1980, he conducted political education forums and wrote an influential pamphlet entitled "Vote Maturely," calling on Ugandans to resist dictatorship and support free and fair elections.[24] The Ugandan people indeed voted, and early returns showed an apparent victory for the Catholic-dominated Democratic Party (DP). But factions in the military rigged the final outcome to ensure the victory of Obote and the Uganda People's Congress (UPC).[25] In the aftermath, the country descended into a scorched-earth civil war between Obote's government and Yoweri Museveni's National Resistance Army (NRA). Waliggo wrote clandestinely during the war and likely had a hand in some of the Catholic bishops' or Uganda Episcopal Conference's hardest-hitting pastoral letters such as "I Have Heard the Cry of My People" (1980), "Be Converted and Live" (1981), and "In God We Trust" (1982).[26] Frustrated with the DP, Ugandan Catholics' historical political movement, he also became a clandestine supporter of the NRA during the bush war. As recounted at the beginning of this chapter, Obote's agents sought to arrest him in January 1983, and Waliggo fled into exile.

Waliggo remained in exile in Nairobi, Kenya, for most of the next four years. During this period, he taught at the newly founded Catholic Higher Institute of Eastern Africa, later renamed the Catholic University of East Africa, where he served as the first chair of the Department of Church History and general editor of *African Christian Studies*, a journal that grew into one of the leading organs of African theology on the continent.[27] But Waliggo always intended to return to Uganda when the political situation

24. Mayanja, interview; Waliggo and Mayanja, *Political Education*. As Mayanja recounted, the authors' counsel in this document has been ignored in postcolonial Uganda: "A soldier has never been meant to rule but to fight."

25. Kasozi, *Social Origins of Violence*, 143.

26. Ssettuuma, interview, July 6, 2017. For his part, Mayanja sees the Comboni Tarcisio Agostoni as having a more decisive impact on the pastoral letters of the 1980s. Waliggo associates concur that he was a primary drafter of pastoral letters on political themes in the 1990s and early 2000s, and Waliggo also drafted statements for Adrian Ddungu, his own bishop in Masaka diocese (Mayanja, interview; Sserwanga, interview).

27. Magesa, "Theological Legacy of John Mary Waliggo," 80–82.

improved. After reading several of his works, including "Vote Maturely," Museveni sought a clandestine meeting with Waliggo in 1984. After taking power in 1986, Museveni convinced Waliggo to contribute to Uganda's process of revising the 1967 constitution.

Waliggo became one of the key players in Uganda's constitutional revision, a popular process unlike any the country—and even the continent—had seen to that point.[28] As a commissioner between 1989 and 1993, he crisscrossed Uganda's eastern province, conducting public forums in which he dialogued with thousands of Ugandans and sought popular input on constitutional priorities.[29] Waliggo supplemented this roadwork with daily radio call-in shows on constitutionalism.[30] He was also the primary drafter of UEC pastoral letters on the constitutional process, such as "Towards a New National Constitution" (1989) and "Political Maturity: Consolidating Peace and National Unity in Uganda" (1995).[31] After the Constituent Assembly was launched in 1993, Waliggo was named as secretary. Working with a small team of seminarians, he reduced the 8,000-page draft constitution to a feasible 800 pages, taking refuge again in the Ssese Islands to complete this herculean task in a mere two months in 1994.[32]

After the promulgation of the constitution in 1995 and democratic elections in 1996, Waliggo planned to step back from public life. But President Museveni convinced him to stay on at Uganda's new Human Rights Commission (UHRC), a group Waliggo had pushed for in the constitution. At the UHRC, Waliggo oversaw the Education, Training, and Research Division.[33] In this role, he instituted new human rights curricula for schools and, even more critically, human rights training for Uganda's security services (e.g., police, army, prisons, and intelligence services). Waliggo

28. In the words of Aili Tripp, "rarely in Africa has one seen the level of popular engagement in education seminars, debates, media discussions, and submission of memoranda such as was evident during the Ugandan constitution-making process . . . At least 25,547 separate submissions of views were sent to the commission" (Tripp, *Museveni's Uganda*, 78).

29. Overall, around 30,000 Ugandan community leaders participated in constitutional seminars during this time (Tripp, *Museveni's Uganda*, 79).

30. Kaggwa, interview.

31. Nanseera, interview; Rweza, interview. Waliggo also likely had a hand in the 2005 UEC statement, "Towards a Democratic and Peaceful Uganda Based on the Common Good."

32. Ssettuuma, interview, July 6, 2017. For Waliggo's own synopsis of the constitutional process, see Waliggo, "Some Key Lessons."

33. Uganda Human Rights Commission, "1997 Annual Report," 4.

focused in particular on sensitizing security personnel to the problem of torture.[34] In this regard, one of his lasting legacies was the development and promulgation of a human rights training manual for Uganda's police. In 1999 alone, the UHRC trained over 1,400 police in "rights-based policing," and human rights desks were soon established in the police, army, and prisons.[35] Shortly thereafter, human rights became an examinable subject in police training.[36] As Waliggo and his colleagues noted, "the development of human rights training manuals for the security organs is a major achievement given that these organs have historically been the major human rights abusers in the country."[37] In his work at the UHRC, Waliggo also showed an ability to see ahead, helping commissioners reach consensus on non-discrimination against homosexuals years before the issue exploded in Uganda's public sphere.[38]

Even as he spearheaded Uganda's human rights work, Waliggo maintained a hectic schedule as a priest and scholar, including teaching at Uganda Martyrs University and Kenya's Tangaza University; chairing the Ugandan National Diocesan Priests' Conference; serving as deputy national executive secretary of the National Catholic Commission for Justice and Peace; conducting a weekly radio show; and writing and speaking to innumerable Catholic communities and other Christian groups across the country.[39] After a life of surprisingly good health, he fell suddenly ill in 2007 and was diagnosed with stomach cancer. Although some friends speculate he may have been poisoned due to his sensitive work with the UHRC, a more likely cause was his lifelong chain-smoking habit. His initial cancer treatments went well in both Uganda and South Africa. Tragically, however, he died on April 19, 2008, on a flight from South Africa to Uganda, likely killed by a

34. Sekaggya, interview.

35. Uganda Human Rights Commission, "Annual Report 1999," 23; Uganda Human Rights Commission, "6th Annual Report 2003," xiii, 27; Saboni, "Uganda Human Rights Commission."

36. Kamya, interview.

37. Uganda Human Rights Commission, "Annual Report January 2001–September 2002," 42.

38. Byamukama, interview. Uganda gained international notoriety after its parliament passed a bill in 2009 that instituted severe punishments for "aggravated homosexuality." The bill was signed into law in a modified form in 2014 (Van Klinken, "Christianity and Same-Sex Relationships," 494).

39. Kanyandago, "John Mary Waliggo," 218; Sekaggya, "Eulogy."

blood clot induced by his cancer medications.[40] He was buried at Bukalasa Minor Seminary, the place where his grandmother had first raised priests who could fight slavery.

Ten Key Themes in Waliggo's Theology of Liberation

One of the pleasures of John Mary Waliggo's writings is his gift for structure and organization. In the words of one former colleague, "he could give a systematic and comprehensive response to almost any question."[41] In turn, many of his writings originated as oral speeches, and he was accustomed to audiences with limited time and short attention spans. Reflecting these settings, most of his papers include numbered bullet lists breaking down the most essential points of his argument. So to borrow not just the substance but also the form of Waliggo, I present here the top ten dimensions of Waliggo's theology of liberation.

1. **Liberation is the heart of the gospel message.** For Waliggo, God's incarnation, death, and resurrection in Jesus Christ should liberate humans from all that oppresses and instills fear. Like so many victims in today's world, Christ was rejected and discarded by the religious and political powers of his time. But the cross and resurrection are ultimately signs of God's vindication of Christ and all of the victims of the world. "The rejected Jesus of Nazareth, being raised from the dead as the victorious Christ, to the great shame and dismay of his rejecters, is the Christ that is relevant to Africa."[42] For Waliggo, now that Christ has set us free, we must dedicate our lives to freeing others from all that oppresses them. Perhaps even more importantly, we must recognize our own intrinsic human dignity and need to actively liberate ourselves from all that is keeping us from flourishing. This is why Waliggo argued that the "root cause of all injustice in Africa" was not first and foremost bad political leadership, inequality, or neocolonialism, but people's "ignorance of their God-given dignity and human rights."[43] In this regard, Galatians 5:1 was one of Waliggo's favorite

---

40. Rweza, interview.

41. Kituuma, interview.

42. Waliggo, quoted in Kanyandago, "John Mary Waliggo," 224.

43. Waliggo, "Evaluation of Catholic Social Teaching," 1173.

verses: "It is for freedom that Christ has set us free. Stand firm, then, and do not let yourselves be burdened again by the yoke of slavery."[44]

2. **Liberation must be integral.** Waliggo rejected both a materialism that denied the spiritual dimension of human existence and a spiritualism that denied the embodied, material nature of human life. For Waliggo, liberation was a polyvalent concept with ten key dimensions:[45]

- *spiritual liberation*, namely by bringing the person closer to God and neighbor, especially through the ability to engage in spontaneous prayer;

- *moral liberation*, helping people to make mature moral decisions by recognizing their complicity in social sin (and not only interpersonal or sexual sins);

- *religious liberation*, enabling people to freely seek God out of conviction rather than fear;

- *mental liberation*, fighting ignorance and fatalism through educating and empowering common people to brainstorm solutions to their own situations of deprivation;[46]

- *cultural liberation*, namely by struggling against any form of cultural domination, especially the tendency for the West to impose its monoculture on Africa;

- *economic liberation*, struggling in solidarity with the poor to help them achieve a humane standard of living;

- *political liberation* through liberating people from authoritarian domination;

- *physical liberation*, especially through meeting people's bodily needs and restoring a healthy ecological relationship with the land;

- *social liberation* through fighting isolationism, racism, individualism, tribalism, and other forms of collective discrimination; and

---

44. Ssettuuma, interview, July 6, 2017.

45. The following list is adapted from Waliggo's own explanation in Ssettuuma, *Thief on the Plane*, 65–67.

46. Waliggo here draws directly on Freire, *Pedagogy of the Oppressed*. He notes elsewhere that he studied Freire's thought extensively during his mid-1980s exile period in Kenya (Waliggo, "Link between Violence, Insecurity, and Poverty," 973).

- *personal liberation* by realizing one's God-given human dignity and becoming a "protagonist for liberation"[47] for others.

Such a multifaceted concept of liberation is difficult if not impossible to fully achieve but no less important for that. As Waliggo commented to one of his nephews, "Unless a person is liberated holistically, [something] will come back to haunt you."[48]

3. **Liberative politics is about furthering justice and life.** Waliggo defined politics as the "art or skills of organizing people and influencing them to work for the common good."[49] He consistently argued that a liberative politics should be oriented around the fundamental African value of life, arguing that a "pro-life" and "pro-people" politics should prioritize peace, human rights, democracy, integral development, and environmental protection.[50] He also spent his life advocating for justice in both the church and society. In the words of one of his former mentees, "He was always on the side of the oppressed, especially those who have no voice."[51]

4. **The Church has an important role to play in public and political life since its holistic mission affects the entire human person.** At the ascension, the angels told Jesus's disciples not to stare at the sky but to return to Jerusalem to proclaim the gospel (Acts 1:10–11). For Waliggo, the Ugandan Church has had a similar tendency to overly "spiritualize" and "eschatologize" life's challenges. Rather, the Church's task is to "concretize salvation," seeking to further life and liberation in the here and now.[52] This does not obviate the Christian's hope for eternal life, but this hope should serve as a motivation for current engagement rather than, to echo Marx, as an "opiate" that drugs a person and prevents her from struggling against the oppressive structures of her own historical moment. Waliggo therefore argued that

47. Ssettuuma, *Thief on the Plane*, 67.

48. Nanseera, interview.

49. Waliggo, "Church and Politics in the Second Independence," 468.

50. Waliggo, "Development of Religious Life," 259; Waliggo, "Some Key Lessons," 704.

51. Kituuma, interview.

52. Ssettumma Jr., interview, July 6, 2017; Waliggo, "Challenging Vision." Eschatology here refers to future hopes and horizons, especially the "end times" and Christian expectations for God's final judgment and reign.

the Church's "evangelization must be integral, Christianizing every dimension of life."[53]

5. **The Church's political engagement should support the liberative politics that Waliggo envisions for all of society.** In Waliggo's understanding, the Church is first and foremost "all the people of God, all the baptized people,"[54] and the "politics of the church" is about liberation and life. In this regard, the Church should neither be privatized, nor should its public role be confused with that of the state. Rather, the Church has a special role to play in promoting values of forgiveness and reconciliation and encouraging human rights for the marginalized and vulnerable.[55] The Church also has a responsibility to support democracy, namely to "carry out a critical analysis of society, to play a more active role in the democratization process, and to empower people, especially the ordinary people and the disadvantaged, to become the primary actors in the democratization process."[56]

6. **The Church's relationship with the State should be prophetic but not adversarial.** The Church's role is not to replace the state or to carve out its own alternative space as a "demonstration plot" to the kingdom of God.[57] Nor should the clergy become denominational or political partisans, dividing parties between those of "God and Satan."[58] The church as prophet should not fear to condemn the ills of society, but it should also collaborate with the government whenever possible. For Waliggo, one of the church's public tasks is to inculcate the value of patriotism, a commitment to serving the good of the nation. This explains in part why he spent so much of his public life serving in government corridors. As he told a close friend, "While I am there [in

53. Waliggo, "Major Challenges to Catholic Missionaries," 281.

54. Waliggo, "Church and Politics in Conflict Resolution," 457. Here Waliggo is following Vatican II's description of the Church as "the people of God" in the second chapter of *Lumen Gentium*.

55. For Waliggo, the marginalized included women, children, persons with disabilities, refugees, the elderly, the sick, the poor, and the illiterate. On Waliggo's vision of children's rights, including rights to life, responsible parenthood, education, protection from abuse, and medical care, see Waliggo, "Children's Rights in the New Constitution," 1125–33.

56. Waliggo, "Major Challenges to Catholic Missionaries," 280.

57. The latter vision has been propagated by one of Waliggo's former students, Emmanuel Katongole (Katongole, *Sacrifice of Africa*, 180).

58. Waliggo, "Priests and Politics," 480.

government], let me be the candle."[59] This also points to the greatest
ambiguity surrounding Waliggo's legacy, namely his close association
of "pro-life, pro-people" politics with the NRM and his concomitant
failure to publicly critique or distance himself from Museveni's government in his later years.

7. **If the state becomes a dictatorship, the prophetic Church must
embrace a Theology of Revolution & Last Resort.** If he were alive
today, Waliggo would likely be a fan of the most recent trilogy of *Star
Wars* films. For the politics of liberation always entails *resistance* to
the negative values of cruel and tyrannical politics, which for Waliggo
included ignorance, elitism, intolerance, prejudice, poverty, underde-
velopment, dictatorship, corruption, war, armed conflict, terrorism,
and cultural oppression.[60] If people are being oppressed, they have the
right to defend themselves in a spirit of "holy anger."[61] Although he
did not take up arms, Waliggo offered clandestine material support
for the NRA during the 1980s civil war and subsequently wrote of the
Church's need to develop a "theology of last resort" and a "theology
of revolution" to complement traditional just-war thinking.[62] Here
Waliggo shared some Latin American liberation theologians' support
for armed violence in situations of political oppression and dictatorship, a door that had been opened ever so slightly by Pope Paul VI in
Populorum Progressio.[63]

8. **Inculturation should be shaped by a lens of liberation.** One of
the primary currents of postcolonial African theology has been the
turn to inculturation. This aims to make Christianity more genuinely
"African" by rehabilitating indigenous cultural and religious values,
finding God in traditional culture, and liberating the kernel of Jesus's

59. Wasswa Mpagi, interview.

60. Waliggo, "Education for Resistance," 508.

61. Ssettuuma, interview, July 6, 2017.

62. Author's field notes, Kampala, Uganda, June 24, 2015; Waliggo, "Church and the
Revolutionary Process." According to Patrick Bugembe, Waliggo broke from DP in the
1980s to support the NRA because the latter wanted to overthrow the political system
rather than just work within it like DP (Bugembe, interview).

63. "We know, however, that a revolutionary uprising—save where there is manifest,
long-standing tyranny which would do great damage to fundamental personal rights and
dangerous harm to the common good of the country—produces new injustices, throws
more elements out of balance and brings on new disasters. A real evil should not be
fought against at the cost of greater misery" (Paul VI, *Populorum Progressio*, sec. 31).

good news from the husk of Western cultural imperialism. Waliggo strongly supported the theology of inculturation, seeing this movement as crucial to a "marriage of Christianity and culture" that would enable Christianity to become "relevant to the people."[64] But he also argued that genuine inculturation needed to be "liberative," "progressive," and "dynamic," rejecting both fatalism and traditional Ugandan patriarchy that discriminated against women, children, and the disabled.[65] Here Waliggo was very critical of traditional practices like female circumcision, polygamy, the exclusion of women from land inheritance, and an overall "culture of oppressive silence," especially women's and children's silence in the presence of men.[66] In Waliggo's words, "culture, in whatever manner, cannot and should not be above or against justice. Whatever enslaves, oppresses, and dehumanizes a person or a section of society must be uprooted and replaced by the values of justice, equality and human dignity."[67]

9. **The Church's commitment to liberation should be an ecumenical venture.** As one of Uganda's premier church historians, Waliggo was well aware of the checkered political and religious history of Catholic-Anglican-Muslim relations in precolonial and colonial Uganda. Religious competition had produced much discord in both his family's and his country's history—for example, his Muslim grandfather had tried to force his Catholic grandmother to become a Muslim.[68] Not surprisingly, for Waliggo the modern ecumenical movement is crucial to the liberation of the church from destructive patterns of identity politics and denominational rivalry. Christians should also collaborate across denominational lines to support political justice, patriotism, and democratization, as Waliggo did in 1980 when he formed the interreligious "Better World Movement" to advocate for human rights and free and fair elections.[69]

---

64. Sserwanga, interview.

65. Waliggo, "Task of Inculturation," 1012–20.

66. Waliggo, "Cultural Practices, Customs, and Traditions," 681. Women's rights were not a peripheral issue for Waliggo who, late in his career, wrote an entire book on the subject (Waliggo, *Struggle for Equality*).

67. Waliggo, *Man of Vision*, 38.

68. Kanyandago, "John Mary Waliggo," 217.

69. Ssettuuma, *Thief on the Plane*, 43.

10. **Memory—and thus history—are critical to liberation theology.** Finally, although historians and theologians tend to see themselves occupying wholly separate scholarly spheres, Waliggo saw his historical research as a crucial dimension of his theopolitical project of liberation. Exploitative political regimes aim to cultivate communal amnesia and historical romanticism. To counter this, historians should pursue a "history from the grassroots . . . a people-centered history, which takes into account the cries and pains of the existential situation of the people."[70] For Waliggo, the critical task of the church historian stems from the degree to which our recollection of the oppressive past helps us to create a more liberating present and future.[71] To close with his words, "Every human person and especially every Christian must be a person who remembers. It is in remembering that we continually discover our liberation by God from all types of slavery, oppression, and suppression. We also discover the men and women God uses in our liberation."[72]

The Priest in Public:
The Leadership Legacies of Fr. John Mary Waliggo

What lessons can we draw from Waliggo's witness as a pastoral leader and public theologian? First, for all of his intellectual and civic achievements, Waliggo is best remembered by his friends for his simplicity, humility, generosity, love for life, and his care for his fellow priests and ordinary parishioners. In the words of his former classmate, Msgr. Joseph Kasule, "[Waliggo] could approach any person. He never showed in his life that he was a 'big man.'"[73] For Fr. Herman Kituuma, rector of Katigondo National Seminary, Waliggo embodied the African proverb that "a good leader has four ears. He can listen to the lowest person and the highest person."[74] Margaret Sekaggya, Waliggo's former supervisor at the Uganda Human

---

70. Waliggo, quoted in Ssettuuma, *Thief on the Plane*, 30. See also Waliggo, "Ecumenism in Uganda."

71. Kituuma, interview.

72. Waliggo, "Christian Ethics and Leadership," 885.

73. Kasule, interview. Nathan Byamukama, who worked with Waliggo as a junior staffer at the UHRC, likewise highlighted Waliggo's ability to move freely with all staff. "He always wanted to be even with you, not over you" (Byamukama, interview).

74. Kituuma, interview.

Rights Commission, noted how he once personally paid a three-cow bride price to free a woman from an abusive marriage.[75] His longtime secretary, Elizabeth Bosa, also highlighted his counseling for married couples, refugees, and fellow priests.[76] In his final years, so many people visited Waliggo at home that his roommate, Fr. Zachary Rweza, used to kid him, "You have killed my privacy!"[77] To echo Pope Francis, one of Waliggo's important legacies of leadership is simply the way he comported himself as a joyful and authentic evangelizer who rubbed shoulders with regular people and "took on the smell of his sheep."[78]

Second, Waliggo embodies both the promises and the pitfalls of the African priest as public servant. In general, African priests wear far more hats than their Western counterparts. In addition to sacramental ministry, the priest is often a community mediator, liaison for international development aid, and civic activist. In many ways, Waliggo nationalized this understanding of the local priest as civic leader. Although he embraced parish ministry and lauded participatory democracy at the local level,[79] his newspaper columns and radio programs reached a national audience, and he spoke frequently to religious and civic forums around Uganda and the region. He even referred to himself as the unofficial "chaplain of Parliament."[80] Like Reinhold Niebuhr or Martin Luther King Jr. in the American context, he was a public theologian in the public square (and even here it is difficult to imagine King or Niebuhr revising the national constitution or heading a government commission). For Waliggo, to be a priest meant being a defender of human rights. As he commented to a friend, "this is also ministry. If I am not here to see human rights are observed in the country, what am I doing as a priest? We must fight injustice."[81]

After 1986, Waliggo's national activism entailed a very close relationship with Museveni and the ruling NRM government. For example, he did not publicly support the 1999 referendum to reintroduce multiparty politics, and he did not publicly oppose the constitutional change that enabled

75. Sekaggya, interview.

76. Bosa, interview.

77. Rweza, interview.

78. Francis, *Evangelii Gaudium*, sec. 24.

79. Waliggo, "Synopsis of the State of Constitutional Struggle," 720.

80. Nanseera, interview.

81. Kamya, interview.

Museveni to run for a third term in 2006.[82] President Museveni even paid for his extensive medical bills at the end of his life.[83] This is not to say that Waliggo refrained from all critique of government policies or behavior. More socialist in his own economic thinking, he was always uncomfortable with the NRM's embracing of neo-liberal capitalism.[84] In 1999, he criticized NRA corruption, lack of transparency, and wartime abuses in northern Uganda, arguing (in an NRM journal no less) that "the right to peace and security for citizens of parts of the north and west has not been guaranteed . . . the right to personal liberty has been undermined by over-enthusiastic agents of the State, under the unacceptable excuse of cracking down on terrorism and lawlessness."[85] Like Cardinal Nsubuga, Waliggo also believed that genuine results were achieved through behind-the-scenes engagement and "quiet diplomacy" rather than public confrontation.[86] But given his moral stature, one wonders whether Waliggo should have distanced himself more publicly from the government, especially during the final decade of his life when Museveni's and the NRM's authoritarian tendencies became ever more evident.[87] As one of his friends recalled, "he went into politics and found it hard to come out."[88] One recalls here the cautions of Pope Benedict XVI in *Africae Munus*: "To yield to the temptation to become political leaders or social agents would be to betray your priestly ministry and to do a disservice to society, which expects of you prophetic words and deeds."[89]

Third, Waliggo's life witness and his political theology are ultimately about countering the politics of fear. As he experienced in his own life, God's liberating grace pierces the fears that silence or paralyze us, preventing us and our society from flourishing to our full human potential. This

82. Rweza, interview. For Waliggo's views on the 1999 multiparty referendum (which ultimately passed), see Waliggo, "How Constitutional is this Referendum?"

83. Bosa, interview; Sekaggya, "Eulogy."

84. Bugembe, interview.

85. Waliggo, "New Constitution and New Approaches," 701–2.

86. Kaggwa, interview; Bosa, interview. For Kaggwa, such public confrontation is politically ineffective in the African context, especially as religious figures are not expected to assume the roles of opposition leaders.

87. In the 2001 presidential elections, opposition candidate Kizza Besigwe was beaten and forced to flee the country, and he was placed under house arrest during and after the 2006 election (Reid, *History of Modern Uganda*, 83).

88. Unattributable interview.

89. Benedict XVI, *Africae Munus*, sec. 108.

also entails countering a type of spiritual fatalism that accepts whatever happens as "God's will." In a twenty-first-century context of growing identity politics, which often plays out in the fearful and angry scapegoating of immigrants, there is need now more than ever for a public theology of hope, hospitality, and life. Such a public theology recognizes that God calls us to a radical love of neighbor that crosses ethnic, national, and party lines.[90] It demonstrates that, in Waliggo's words, the "struggle for justice is also the struggle for peace." And it encourages Christians to work for democratic structures based on principles of justice, equality, accountability, and freedom, especially for the socially marginalized, such as women, the disabled, the poor, and the illiterate.[91] Ultimately, Waliggo's public theology is oriented around what he sees as the heart of the African worldview: a politics of life that reflects God's will for life.

> *"Whatever promotes life, transmits life, manifests life, enriches life, saves life, protects life, ensures life, heals life, is good and must be longed for by all. Whatever does the opposite is evil and must be avoided by all."*[92]

Reflection Questions

1. What images or words do you associate with "liberation?" Which of Waliggo's components of liberation theology resonate the most with you?

2. From what do you, your church, and/or your community need "liberation?"

3. Given his primary vocation as a Catholic priest, was Fr. Waliggo too involved in national political life? Why or why not?

4. What do you see as the priest's ideal public role in your own local community, especially in relationship to Catholic social teaching?

90. Magesa highlights Waliggo's strident opposition to ethnic segregation, even among his fellow Baganda, during their shared years teaching at the Catholic Higher Institute of Eastern Africa (Magesa, "Theological Legacy," 81).

91. Waliggo, "Christian Ethics and Leadership," 885–89.

92. Waliggo, "Role of Culture and Religion in Authentic Development," 933.

4

Solidarity on the Streets
Sr. Rose Mystica Muyinza

AT THE AGE OF thirteen, Justine Babirye's life was spiraling out of control. The child of Rwandan migrants who had fled their home country during the Hutu revolution of 1959–1962, Justine lost her father during Uganda's civil war in the early 1980s. She and her siblings were left to fend for themselves. At age thirteen, Justine found herself in a refugee camp in Toro in western Uganda, one of the innumerable "Luweero Triangle girls" who had been displaced and orphaned during the war. Shortly after Yoweri Museveni's National Resistance Army (NRA) came to power in January 1986, Justine found her way to Kampala. A friend suggested that she visit the Daughters of Charity home near the Nile Hotel in downtown Kampala. Here she encountered the tall, warm presence of Sr. Rose Mystica Muyinza. When she saw Babirye, Sr. Rose opened her arms, hugged her, and cried out, "Justine, now I am going to be your mother! You will have so many sisters and brothers here!" Babirye lived at the Daughters of Charity (DoC) home for the better part of the next decade. Through DoC, she finished her secondary schooling and went on to study public administration and health policy at the university level. Today she and her husband run Keith Associates, an agrochemical business in downtown Kampala. Justine attributes all of her professional success, and even her survival, to the woman she affectionately calls "Aunt Rose." "I cherish my life and who I am today because of her! I would have died of HIV without her."[1]

---

1. Babirye, interview.

FIGURE 7

Justine Babirye's encounter with Sr. Rose Muyinza reflects a Catholic ethos I describe as "solidarity on the streets." I borrow the term *solidarity* from the tradition of Catholic social teaching, namely the call to remember that we are members of one human family, our dignity originating in our creation in the *imago Dei* (Gen 1:27–28). Solidarity reflects humans' fundamentally communal and relational nature as "social beings"; we are not autonomous individuals but people called to find our freedom in self-giving relationship with others. In the words of the *Compendium of the Social Doctrine of the Church*, "Solidarity highlights in a particular way the intrinsic social nature of the human person, the equality of all in dignity and rights, and the common path of individuals and peoples towards an ever more committed unity."[2] Solidarity also entails a ministry of presence, walking with people and sharing their life. In the words of Pope St. John

2. Pontifical Council of Justice and Peace, *Compendium of the Social Doctrine*, sec. 193.

Paul II, solidarity "is not a feeling of vague compassion or shallow distress at the misfortunes of so many people, both near and far. On the contrary, it is a firm and persevering determination to commit oneself to the common good; that is to say to the good of all and of each individual, because we are all really responsible for all."[3]

When I say "the streets," however, I am veering away from the rarefied discourse of Catholic theology and into the tangled world of English slang. The Longman Dictionary of Contemporary English defines "the streets" as "the busy public parts of a city where there is a lot of activity, excitement, and crime, or where people without homes live."[4] Even more provocative are the definitions included in the online Urban Dictionary. Here "street" and "streets" are variously described as "where the poor urban ghetto people live"; "being able to pick up on all things quickly"; "relating to all types of people"; "the opposite of *bourgeois*—'street' implies hustle"; and "the cold reality of day-to-day life and achieving."[5] In summary, "streets" connotes poverty and the social margins, yet also refers to ingenuity, energy, accessibility, and thinking outside the box. In other words, we are talking about living with the poor, yet also bringing creative passion to tackling the root causes of social marginalization.

So, if we bring these two dimensions together to form the idea of "solidarity on the streets," what do we have? First, "solidarity on the streets" entails *relocating to the streets*. In this regard, solidarity involves not just a "feeling of vague compassion,"[6] as John Paul II notes. Rather, it entails an embodied commitment to those on the margins, a commitment perhaps best embodied in physical relocation. To quote the African-American Christian activist John Perkins, "Relocation is incarnation . . . Living involvement turns poor people from statistics into our friends."[7] Such a commitment reflects an incarnational vision of God as one who, to paraphrase John 1:14, "pitched his tent with us" in the person of Jesus Christ. This vision also draws on Pope Francis's well-known calls for the church to leave the security of the sacristy to encounter the "suffering flesh of others."[8]

---

3. John Paul II, *Sollicitudo Rei Socialis*, sec. 38.

4. Longman Dictionary of Contemporary English, "Streets," lines 1–2.

5. Urban Dictionary, "Street," lines 6–8, 13–14.

6. John Paul II, *Sollicitudo Rei Socialis*, sec. 38.

7. See Perkins, "CCDA 2006 Dr. John Perkins," 44:55. See also Marsh, *Beloved Community*, 174.

8. Francis, *Evangelii Gaudium*, sec. 24.

In Pope Francis's words, "I prefer a Church which is bruised, hurting and dirty because it has been out on the streets rather than a Church which is unhealthy from being confined and from clinging to its own security."[9] In other words, Catholic leaders living out an incarnational ministry are not seeking comfort but embodying compassion. For the theologian Henri Nouwen, this movement of compassion is one of "voluntary displacement," namely moving "from the ordinary and proper places to the places where they could experience and express their compassionate solidarity with those in whom the brokenness of the human condition was most visible."[10]

Second, solidarity on the streets entails advocacy, or *speaking from the streets*. To echo the Jesuits, if relocating embodies the "man or woman *with* others," speaking from the streets points to the need for "men and women *for* others."[11] Faithful shepherds should live in solidarity with their sheep. But typically they have also benefited from higher educational opportunities, wider professional networks, and greater financial resources than most of their sheep. In amplifying the voices of the voiceless, effective Catholic leaders serve as advocates who can draw much-needed attention and resources to the social and human challenges in their midst.

Third, solidarity on the streets ultimately aims to *transform the streets*. In my own home city of Omaha, one of the most successful urban ministries is run by an evangelical Christian group called Abide Ministries. Abide defines itself as "an inner-city, non-profit organization with a dream that one day, Omaha, Nebraska would have no inner city."[12] Like Abide, the fruitful Christian leader does not leave the situation the way she found it but helps transform the community to better reflect Jesus's inauguration of an already-but-not-yet reign of God. At the same time, the faithful Catholic leader is not a messiah figure who simply rescues people. Rather, the most effective and long-lasting changes will be carried forward by the people

9. Francis, *Evangelii Gaudium*, 49.

10. McNeill et al., *Compassion*, 68. The authors see voluntary displacement as the seed of "all great religious reforms," whether the monastic movement of Benedict of Nursia, the mendicant movement of St. Francis of Assisi, or Dorothy Day's Catholic Worker.

11. Emphasis mine. The language originated with the former superior general of the Jesuits, Pedro Arrupe, SJ (Arrupe, "Men for Others").

12. As stated on Abide's website, "our mission is to revitalize the inner city, one neighborhood at a time" (Abide, "Our Mission"). Their actual pastoral approach is even more "micro," working on a street-by-street basis with local neighbors to build up families, neighborhood communities, and housing (Dotzler, interview). On the vision of Abide and their founder Rev. Ron Dotzler, see his appropriately titled *Out of the Seats and into the Streets*.

themselves, and the best Christian leaders will empower local people to do just this. To paraphrase Augustine of Hippo, "God does not save us without us."

In this chapter, I will tell the story of Sr. Rose Muyinza's radical life and creative apostolate through this lens of "solidarity on the streets" and its trifold dimensions of relocation, advocacy, and transformation. Sr. Rose's life and apostolate were intertwined at every step of her journey. Such will be our approach in this chapter.

Solidarity on the Streets: The Life Witness of Sr. Rose Muyinza

Rose Muyinza was born in Seeta in April 1935 into a wealthy family who owned significant properties in Mukono district in south-central Uganda.[13] The daughter of devout Anglicans, she showed early signs of her independent personality by choosing to become a Catholic. She did so after determining that Catholicism offered a surer path to holiness for a Muganda woman; as a young girl she had been advised by a local man to "become a nun if you want to get to heaven."[14] She studied at an Nkokonjeru primary school run by the Little Sisters of St. Francis and later at Mt. St. Mary's Namagunga where she displayed affinities for math, music, dance, and drama. After finishing secondary school in 1954, she entered the novitiate of the Little Sisters of St. Francis. Started by the Irish missionary Mother Kevin Kearney in 1923, the Little Sisters were one of the first indigenous women's religious communities in East Africa. They also grew to become one of the largest in the region.[15] Mother Kevin envisioned the Little Sisters as a contemplative community that would also engage in a medical apostolate, especially as maternal and pediatric nurses. As time progressed, they also embraced an educational apostolate, outreach to the poor, and ministry to the physically and mentally handicapped.[16]

13. General biographical information is drawn from Mugisa, "Daughters of Charity Founder," 4.

14. Nalwanga, "Sister Muyinza," 1.

15. The Little Sisters and the Ugandan Church have championed Mother Kevin's cause for sainthood; she was recently named a "Servant of God." Today the Little Sisters number more than 700 in Uganda alone, and they have additional communities in Rwanda, Burundi, Kenya, Tanzania, and the USA.

16. Kollman and Toms Smedley, *Understanding World Christianity*, 231; Namuddu and D'Arbela, "Congregation of the Little Sisters," 111–25; Mary Cleophas, interview.

She may have become a nun to get to heaven, but ultimately Sr. Rose did not find earthly fulfillment with the Little Sisters of St. Francis. Her journey in religious life began well enough. She completed her novitiate and professed her initial vows, and in 1956 the congregation sent her to study education at Kampala's famous Makerere University. However, Sr. Rose was so exasperated with her education studies that she lost her voice, a condition that was later determined to be psychosomatic.[17] As her frustrations mounted, she convinced her reluctant superiors to let her switch to a social work course. But the handwriting was on the wall. The Little Sisters were not ready to embark on the kind of radical social apostolate that Sr. Rose had in mind. Likewise, Sr. Rose had an independent streak that would make life difficult in a hierarchical community built around vows of obedience and stability. Family obligations were also pressing on Muyinza. In 1962, one of her brothers died, leaving behind fifteen children. After her superior refused her request to care for these children, she left the Little Sisters,[18] although she maintained amicable relationships with the community and continued to bring children to Nkokonjeru for visits to Mother Kevin's grave.[19] Sr. Rose also continued to embody the public identity of a women's religious, designing her own blue habit and retaining her personal vows of chastity and poverty. After completing her social work studies at Makerere, she took a job working for the Bank of Uganda. But her true passion lay on the streets of Uganda's capital city.

In 1971, Sr. Rose left her banking job to relocate to the streets of Kampala to start what she intended to be a new women's religious congregation called the "Daughters of Charity" (DoC). She chose the title to emphasize a commitment to service and other-centered charity.[20] Refused formal recognition as a new religious congregation—in part due to the complicated way in which she left the Little Sisters—DoC evolved into more of a faith-based NGO. Her organization's initial mission was to care for orphans and to "help young girls who had social problems."[21] These included young women fleeing poverty, sex trafficking, and war; Catholic women who had

17. Nsubuga, Frankline, interview.

18. Ssempereza, "Sr. Muyinza abadde n'omutima."

19. Tegamanyi, interview.

20. As far as we know, Sr. Rose had no relationship with the international Daughters of Charity, a women's religious community founded by St. Vincent de Paul in France in the seventeenth century.

21. Archdiocese of Kampala, "2006 Report," 1.

been dismissed from religious communities; and the mixed-race children of Asians deported by Amin in 1972. Early on, she began providing capital to these women to help them start their own businesses.[22] Within a few years, she had expanded her ministries to include widows, divorcees, and even young boys, although the ministry retained its distinctively feminine title.[23]

During the 1970s and early 1980s, Sr. Rose's ministries were based at two buildings in downtown Kampala, both named after the Virgin Mary: the "Blue House" in Nsambya, a Catholic-dominated neighborhood; and the "Blue Lady Hostel," located in Kampala's downtown Nakasero district near the Nile Hotel. In the mid-to-late 1980s, she partnered with the Italian Consolata Fathers and an affiliated Italian charity named *Insieme Si Puo* to construct three new centers: Kiwanga Charity Home in Mukono east of Kampala, a place for special-needs children named after Mother Kevin; St. Michael Home for street children in Nsambya, Kampala; and the 108-acre Sabina School in Rakai, dedicated to providing education for HIV orphans during the height of the AIDS epidemic.[24] The next decade saw further growth as Sr. Rose established the twenty-five-acre Namugongo Farm, the Bweyogerere mechanical workshop, and the 100-acre Kirinya Boys Land. By the year 2000, it is estimated that "Aunt Rose," as she was affectionately known, had provided direct support for more than 3,000 Ugandan youth.[25] Fittingly, the scriptural quotation that marks the entrance to Kiwanga Center reads "Let the children come unto me" (Mark 10:14). Reflecting her love for its mission to special-needs children, Sr. Rose chose Kiwanga as her burial place. Her grave is a site of frequent popular devotion. Every year, DoC alumni organize a tribute to her on October 8, the day of her death, or October 9, Uganda's independence day.

For all of her public achievements, what friends and beneficiaries most remember about Sr. Rose was her witness of solidarity—in essence, relocating a radical form of religious life to the streets of Uganda. As mentioned above, she maintained a lifelong vow of celibacy, and in public she always wore a simple blue or brown habit. Like an ancient desert ascetic,

22. Nalwanga, "Sister Muyinza," 3.

23. Lubega, interview.

24. Located on a major highway route just north of the Tanzania border in Masaka district, Rakai was "the epicentre of HIV/AIDS in East Africa" (Orobator, *From Crisis to Kairos*, 101).

25. Archdiocese of Kampala, "2006 Report," 1.

she led what one friend described as "a life of self-denial and deprivation,"[26] spending most nights on a six-foot square mattress in her office or sleeping in a bed in the girls' dormitory. She also retained a Catholic sister's emphasis on prayer and discipline. Each of her homes had a residential chapel, and Sr. Rose herself spent part of every Thursday in eucharistic adoration. Even during the worst years of the early-1980s civil war, she never missed 7 a.m. daily mass at nearby Christ the King parish in downtown Kampala. She was known for splashing water on the faces of her girls to wake them for church, driving them in her truck as they belted out their official song, "We are the Daughters of Charity!"[27] Sr. Rose and the Daughters of Charity became fixtures at Christ the King; even today their successors continue to lead a choir at the 7 a.m. Sunday Mass. She also empowered her children to take ownership of their faith, in part by asking children to facilitate morning and evening prayers, lead music, embark on pilgrimages, and provide hospitality for visitors.[28] Yet for all of her emphasis on discipline, former Daughters also recall a life of shared celebration, especially on feast days like Uganda Martyrs.[29] In turn, Sr. Rose's friends describe a woman whose daily prayer practices gave her not just inner consolation, but the clarity of vision and hope to "believe that anything was possible" since it is God who ultimately provides for all.[30]

In relocating to the streets, Sr. Rose was not simply living with the materially poor. Instead, former associates describe her ministry in Luganda as aiding *okuyamba abanaku*—"helping the people without people."[31] In other words, she ministered to all of the socially marginalized groups of her society, including refugees, sex workers, former Catholic sisters or seminarians, the illegitimate children of priests, and special-needs children. In the words of one of her collaborators, Msgr. Charles Kasibante, "her arms were open to all people who needed help," including the unemployed, the elderly, or those facing marital challenges.[32] Her ministry with special-needs children at Kiwanga was especially important given the taboos and superstitions surrounding disabilities in Uganda; one former beneficiary noted how Sr. Rose

26. Kibirango, interview.
27. Nalugo, interview.
28. Birungi, interview; Tegamanyi, interview.
29. Namazzi, interview; Nalugo, interview.
30. Kahooza, interview; Muyingo, interview.
31. Namazzi, interview.
32. Kasibante, interview; Muyingo, interview.

made him far more accepting of persons with disabilities by asking him to work directly with them.[33] Given her own background, Sr. Rose's work with former Catholic nuns or seminarians also stands out. Given Uganda's social stigma surrounding priests or religious who leave consecrated life, Sr. Rose offered these men and women temporary shelter and arranged for counseling, providing a transitional period for them before they rejoined their home communities.[34] To be sure, Sr. Rose worked extensively with the destitute and those lacking the financial means to support themselves; *okuyamba abanaku* can also be translated as "helping the poor." But given the wide range of her ministries, the "woman with a golden heart"[35] is perhaps best described as a "mother of the marginalized." She embodied what the anthropologist China Scherz calls the Kiganda virtue of *omutima omuyambi*, or the "heart for helping" that goes beyond reciprocal family or social obligations to help the "truly needy."[36]

In terms of advocacy and "speaking from the streets," Muyinza was a classic networker and advocate, using her relative privilege and extensive professional connections to attract much-needed funds, volunteers, job opportunities, and public attention for her beloved children. She drew on family relationships, her years working in banking, and her own charisma to develop a remarkable network of local and international advocates. Her network included Leo Kibirango, former president of the Bank of Uganda; First Lady Janet Museveni, with whom she collaborated to start the NGO Uganda Women's Efforts to Save Orphans (UWESO); J. C. Muyingo, later to become the State Minister for Higher Education; and US President Ronald Reagan's daughter, Maureen, who adopted one of the DoC girls. Sr. Rose's honesty, integrity, and direct communication style gave donors confidence in the organization. In the words of her longtime collaborator, Grace Kahooza, "She sacrificed her life for those children. She wasn't there to take the money."[37] In addition to individual private donors and some public-sector contributions, she received support from the Archdiocese of Kampala and

33. Kabuye, interview.

34. Nsubuga, Frankline, interview.

35. Ssempereza, "Sr. Muyinza abadde n'omutima," 1. Muyinza's "big heart" or "golden heart" were also mentioned by other former associates (Muyingo, interview; Mirembe, interview).

36. Scherz, *Having People*, 15, 25. Scherz cites a group of Ugandan Catholic sisters distinguishing between the generic "poor," which would include most Ugandans, and the "truly needy, those who would not be able to do for themselves if we were not here" (83).

37. Kahooza, interview.

invested local Catholic churches in her work, for example by naming Sabina School after the three local parishes from which she adopted children in Rakai district: Sanje, Bisanje, and Nazareth.[38] This extensive support in Uganda provided a foundation for even more lucrative international partnerships, especially with the Italian NGO, *Insieme Si Pro*, and later with the American NGO, Children of Uganda.[39] In addition, Sr. Rose collaborated with the UN's World Food Program and later took the Daughters of Charity choir and dance troupe on multiple fundraising trips to the USA, an innovative idea at the time.[40] In the words of Sr. Theresa Basemera, former caretaker and current Kiwanga administrator, "She could knock anywhere, and they would open."[41]

Her international partnerships could also raise problems for Muyinza. Most grievously, she was arrested and tortured at the Nile Hotel in 1979 during the final months of the Amin dictatorship on suspicion of collaboration with foreign agents.[42] Power struggles with foreign donors could also prove challenging. According to the Archdiocese of Kampala, her partnership with the Italian Catholic charity *Insieme Si Puo* ended in 1996 due to a "misunderstanding."[43] DoC associates were more frank, complaining that these "Italian mafia" were misappropriating money behind the scenes and refusing to share land titles.[44]

The force of Muyinza'a charisma, her vision, and her networking ability carried the Daughters of Charity for over three decades, but the organization hit hard times after Muyinza fell sick with Alzheimer's in 2004. Several colleagues attributed the disease to sleep deprivation and workaholism resulting from an intense schedule of proposal writing, donor meetings, and

38. Ddembe, interview.

39. Kibirango, interview. Although they later pulled back from Sr. Rose's other sites, Children of Uganda retains a close funding relationship with Sabina school, as I discovered when I encountered two American donors conducting an annual visit to the school (Author's field notes, February 2019). On Children of Uganda's mission, see their website, http://childrenofuganda.org.

40. Matovu, interview; Ddembe, interview.

41. Basemera, interview, July 8, 2017.

42. Basemera, interview, July 8, 2017; Nsubuga, Frankline interview. Sr. Rose's reputation for interethnic hospitality may have saved her life. A Lögbara soldier who knew of her ministry on the streets ultimately released her after eleven days of detention.

43. Archdiocese of Kampala, "2006 Report," 2.

44. Birungi, interview. Others placed more blame on the Ugandans that *Insieme Pro* hired in country, claiming they were the ones profiting from property sales (Matovu, interview; Mayanja, interview).

project coordination; one went so far as to say that "she committed suicide in a way."[45] Sr. Rose also kept a tight grip on the Daughters of Charity, to the point that the organization became paralyzed as her own body broke down. "Before Aunt collapsed down, she had been running everything alone . . . Board members had little room to involve in the affairs of the home. This explains why when she fell sick, everything at DOC was at a standstill."[46] Taking advantage of her compromised situation and disorganized record-keeping, several DoC alumni embezzled money and manipulated her to turn over land titles and vehicles to them, which they then sold for personal profit.[47] In the aftermath of this fallout, a longstanding collaboration with a British group known as "Help Uganda" collapsed in 2008,[48] and American donors also pulled back.[49] A decade after her death, there are signs of revitalization. In addition to ongoing partnerships with groups like Children of Uganda, Sabina and its sister institutions at Kiwanga and Nsambya are now operating under new leadership provided by the Archdiocese of Kampala, which, in keeping with Sr. Rose's will, took over DoC properties after her death.[50]

In terms of "transforming the streets," Muyinza demonstrated a special commitment to empowering the young women and men with whom she worked. In the words of the Daughters of Charity's 1993 mission statement, the organization's purpose was "to engage in and carry on non-profit making, non-religious, non-political activities based on love and non-violence with the object of improving the conditions of health, education and training of disadvantaged children."[51] To be sure, Muyinza was a provider of charitable works rather than a political activist for structural change. But her charitable mission went beyond relieving the symptoms of poverty. Instead, Sr. Rose empowered individuals to turn their lives around through giving them the education, life skills, and work experience

45. Babirye, interview.

46. Archdiocese of Kampala, "2006 Report," 2.

47. Kibirango, interview; Babirye interview; Matovu interview; Ssempereza, "Sr. Muyinza abadde n'omutima." For Ssentle, Sr. Rose had a tendency to "overtrust" people, believing that they were as other-centered and genuine as she was (Ssentle, interview).

48. Kibirango, interview.

49. The decline in international funding remained a major concern for staff a decade later (Author's field notes, Sabina School, Rakai, Uganda, February 2019).

50. Basemera interview, July 8, 2017.

51. Archdiocese of Kampala, "2006 Report," 4.

necessary to "send them equipped into society."[52] Toward this end, DoC beneficiaries were trained in catering and small-business entrepreneurship, often spending weekends baking cakes and staffing local weddings. This offered important work experience for young people and helped them to discern their own career paths.[53] It also instilled in them a strong work ethic and an appreciation for self-reliance.[54] Sr. Rose enrolled her children in Uganda's best secondary schools and educated them until they were ready to enter their chosen job fields, even if this meant paying for expensive tertiary education. In Kibarango's words, "she took a community of youth who could not help themselves and turned them into a community that could help themselves."[55] Significantly in a country that continues to struggle with self-described "tribalism" or ethnic favoritism, her reputation was one of "motherly love without discrimination,"[56] welcoming young women and men from all ethnic, class, religious, and national backgrounds. Or as Muyinza said in an interview near the end of her life, her mission was "to serve God's people both within and outside church irrespective of their denomination."[57]

The most eloquent witnesses to Muyinza'a transformative impact are, not surprisingly, the individual Ugandans whom she influenced. Here is just a small sampling of testimonies I received about Sr. Rose's personal impact:

- A native of Jinja, Frankline Mbamanya Nsubuga came to DoC in the late 1980s with two of her sisters. Through DoC, she went on to earn a Makerere University degree in social work. After graduation, she returned to DoC to help the organization improve its counseling and

52. Kahooza, interview. Scherz describes this approach in terms of the "sustainability of a person" rather than the "sustainability of the organization," and she associates this model with Catholic sisters shaped by a similar Franciscan charism to Sr. Rose's Little Sisters of St. Francis (Scherz, *Having People*, 84).

53. Birungi, interview. In turn, successfully catering a couple's wedding earned the couple's good will and often their donations for years to come (Kahooza, interview).

54. Kabuye, interview.

55. Kibirango, interview.

56. Kabuye, interview. Similar sentiments were echoed by Basemera, interview, July 8, 2017; Muyingo, interview; Namazzi, interview.

57. Muyinza, quoted in Nalwanga, "Sister Muyinza," 5. This claim was reinforced by former beneficiaries who described how Sr. Rose ensured that a former Muslim student attended mosque every Friday (Amooti, interview).

childcare practices, and she now coordinates medical research for the HIV program at the Joint Clinical Research Center in Kampala.[58]

- Out of school and working on the streets at the age of nine, Josephine Tegamanyi once walked twelve kilometers barefoot in search of Sr. Rose's home at Nakasero. Entrusted with caring for younger children, she went on to study at a local Consolata Catholic school before completing advanced studies in nursing. She is now a research nurse with a project sponsored by Walter Reed Medical Center.[59]

- Sr. Rose found Tadeo Tebesigwa and his two brothers abandoned in Luwero in the late 1970s. Educated at Nakasero and later Kiwanga, Tadeo chose to come back and dedicate his career to DoC; he has now worked for over twenty years at Sabina as a gardener and chef. Sr. Rose remains his inspiration. "I am 46 years old, and yet I still haven't found someone with the same heart as Sr. Rose."[60]

- In 1992, John Chrysostom Muyingo was struggling to make ends meet on a teacher's salary, and he had little money for his upcoming wedding. He and his bride planned to wed privately in the sacristy of the church. When Sr. Rose found out, she called in Archbishop Emmanuel Wamala to officiate *gratis* and raised sufficient money to fund all other wedding and reception costs. When Muyingo showed up for what he thought would be a private ceremony, all of Rubaga Cathedral was full. Her generosity was a turning point for him, and he vowed to put his money and professional skills toward assisting children in need. Nearly thirty years later, Muyingo is State Minister for Higher Education and supports more than 1,000 children in schools across Uganda. "I am who I am because of that lady!"[61]

- Conceived in a wartime rape and abandoned at birth at Mulago Hospital in 1979, Natal Gloria Birungi was the first of the hundreds of babies adopted through Sr. Rose's "Baby Home" ministry. Encouraged by Sr. Rose to seek her passion, she now works as a professional artist while volunteering with groups like Empower Children Africa and the Rafiki Foundation for widows. "Sr. Rose was my parent, the first

58. Nsubuga, Frankline, interview.
59. Tegamanyi, interview.
60. Tebesigwa, interview.
61. Muyingo, interview.

among my relatives," Birungi says. "She was the Mother Teresa of Uganda!"[62]

Leadership Lessons from "The Mother Teresa of Uganda"

What lessons can we take away from "the Ugandan Mother Teresa?"[63] First, Sr. Rose's radical witness of solidarity on the streets demonstrates the importance of embodied, authentic servant-leadership in the public square. When asked what distinguished Sr. Rose's work from the legions of other charity and development efforts in Uganda, Bishop Paul Ssemogerere commented, "I can liken her to Mother Teresa who would help, not selfishly, but for the sake and the good of the other person."[64] Another former beneficiary said simply, "Today so many people are doing [charity] in a commercial way, but [Sr. Rose] never looked at riches . . . She was rich so long as she satisfied the person in need. She actually was poor!"[65] The insinuation here is that many charitable groups—including many affiliated with Christian churches—are overly profiting from their community work. Yet this also speaks to Muyinza's ability, like Dorothy Day or Mother Teresa of Calcutta, to "take on the smell of the sheep," to trust in God in becoming poor with the poor. To illustrate this, Sabina headmaster Jude Ssentle highlighted how Sr. Rose voluntarily traveled in the back of pickup trucks, gave her bed to visitors, and resisted the substantial African social pressure to present herself as a "big person."[66] Like the namesake of the Little Sisters of St. Francis, Sr. Rose's faith was always embodied in action and service. "Through her actions you could see the love that was flowing."[67]

Second, Sr. Rose and the Daughters of Charity expand our sense of who constitutes "the poor and marginalized." As I mention above, she was described in Luganda as *okuyamba abanaku*, helping the "people without people," "the poor," "the people in need," or even "the abandoned."[68] This

---

62. Birungi, interview.

63. Mugisa, "Daughters of Charity Founder." Other interviewees also used this term to describe Sr. Rose (Kabuye, interview; Muyingo, interview).

64. Ssemogerere, interview.

65. Tebesigwa, interview.

66. Ssentle, interview. Ssentle lamented the absence of this servant leadership model among Uganda's dominant political class.

67. Tegamanyi, interview.

68. Ssemogerere, interview.

category includes the expected groups of the materially destitute, HIV/
AIDS orphans, persons with disabilities, and wartime refugees. But the
category is also surprisingly capacious, reflecting Ugandans' overriding
emphasis on relationships. As one associate pointed out, Sr. Rose's ministry
of *okuyamba abanaku* could extend even to wealthy, "stubborn" children
whose parents had given up on them, often due to poor performance in
school or alcohol or drug addiction.[69] Not surprisingly, "Aunt Rose" built
the Daughters of Charity on the model of a family, reflecting Catholic social
teaching's understanding of solidarity in terms of "one human family" and
the African ecclesiology of the "Church as Family of God."[70] Beneficiaries
were not clients or orphans but "children"; caretakers were "aunts" and
"uncles"; and children were divided into small community "homes" named
after Baby Jesus, St. Michael, and Mother Mary, among others.[71] Importantly, Sr. Muyinza placed no boundaries on who could be accepted into
her communities. In the words of J. C. Muyingo, "her heart went beyond
religion and tribe. Her help was beyond boundaries."[72]

Sr. Rose reminds us, then, that there is something worse than being
materially poor in Uganda—it is being "without people," lacking the trusted
family relationships that constitute our social being-ness. She also reminds
us that the faithful Christian response here is to strive to rebuild kinship.
In the words of the Jesuit Greg Boyle, founder of the gang-rehabilitation
program Homeboy Industries in Los Angeles, "kinship—not serving the
other, but being one with the other. Jesus was not a 'man for others'; he was
one with them."[73]

Finally, Sr. Rose embodies the gifts and challenges of the charismatic
founder. Like Jesus, she had a particular gift for calling disciples. Echoing
Philip's words to Nathanael in John 1:46, she embodied a "come and see"
recruitment strategy that "attracted people to come and work with her," in-
vesting them in relationships that would keep them coming back for years
to come.[74] In many ways, it was her very freedom from and transcending of

69. Amooti, interview.

70. "Church as Family of God" was the dominant ecclesiological image that emerged
from the First African Synod in 1994.

71. Amooti, interview.

72. Muyingo, interview.

73. Boyle, *Tattoos on the Heart*, 188.

74. Kasibante, interview; Amooti, interview. After spending time caring for children,
Amooti left the Apostles of Jesus seminary to work full-time with the Daughters of
Charity.

institutional norms that attracted so many volunteers and donors. In turn, Muyinza's work ethic, entrepreneurial spirit, and motivational skills helped transform DoC from a failed religious congregation into a successful NGO, enabling the Daughters of Charity to become one of Catholic Uganda's most creative street apostolates in the late twentieth century.

Yet the inimitable power of her individual charisma—combined with her resistance to following protocols, her workaholism, and her tendency toward micromanagement—also hindered the long-term sustainability of her movement. In the words of the property manager who took over Kiwanga before her death, "she [Muyinza] had no administrative skills . . . when you start a group without strong administration, you get problems."[75] Related to this was Sr. Rose's restless desire for independence and autonomy. In the words of a former associate, Muyinza "didn't want superiors over her. She wanted to be the boss of her own."[76] In turn, her self-sacrificial spirit and tremendous work ethic ultimately led to physical and mental burnout, contributing to early-onset Alzheimers.[77] In this regard, Sr. Rose offers a cautionary lesson for Catholic community leaders, pointing to the need for rest, self-care, and delegation amidst the constant demands of one's ministry and apostolate. Human beings are finite creatures, and all of us must recognize our limits.

Ultimately, though, it is not Sr. Rose's final years but her decades of solidarity on the streets that are remembered by her friends and former children. In essence, Sr. Rose exemplifies a self-sacrificial servant-leadership marked by a spirit of other-centered *agape,* or self-giving love, sustained by a deep and abiding trust in and affection for God. In the words of her favorite Luganda hymn, *Bwomwewa Omukama,* "When you surrender yourself to the Lord fully, he will never make you lack anything!"

75. Matovu, interview. Mayanja shared this assessment of Sr. Rose as a micromanager: "Everything started with her and ended with her . . . She could appoint you to a job, but she ended up doing it herself" (Mayanja, interview).

76. Nsubuga, Frankline, interview. Msgr. Kasibante also stated that she "maintained a high degree of independence from the church" (Kasibante, interview).

77. In the words of Sabina property manager Joseph Ddembe, "One of the things that made her die was the memory, because she did not have enough time to sleep" (Ddembe, interview).

Reflection Questions

1. Summarize the author's understanding of "solidarity on the streets" in your own words. Who in your life has embodied this type of solidarity?

2. What were the strengths and weaknesses of Sr. Rose's more independent apostolate?

3. Do you think that Sr. Rose overworked herself? Or is this just the price one pays in any dedicated ministry or work?

4. Who are the "people without people" in your own community?

5

Missionaries of the Media

Tonino Pasolini, Sherry Meyer, and Radio Pacis

HUNDREDS OF WELL-WISHERS SURROUNDED the fence at Uganda's Arua airfield as a small Eagle Air prop plane landed on the dusty airstrip. An Italian, an American, and three Ugandans—all leaders of the local Catholic radio station, Radio Pacis—emerged from the aircraft, holding aloft a small trophy. Accompanied by cars, trucks, and boda-boda motorcycles, the Radio Pacis team's journey back to their headquarters became a city-wide festival as thousands of local residents lined the streets singing, dancing, and ululating. Long associated with the dictator Idi Amin, Arua town and West Nile region could now boast of a much different kind of international recognition: Radio Pacis had received the BBC's inaugural 2007 award for the best new radio station in Africa.

In this chapter, I examine Radio Pacis as an example of Catholic social evangelization through media and explore the leadership witness of its missionary founders, Fr. Tonino Pasolini and Ms. Sherry Meyer. In doing so, I shed light on the difficult question of what it means to do fruitful mission in a postcolonial context. The very phrase "postcolonial missionary" can seem anachronistic, given the close association between "colonialism" and "mission" in popular conceptions of Africa.[1] Even in Christian circles, vibrant

---

1. For most American students, this lesson is brought home in their high school reading of Chinua Achebe's *Things Fall Apart*. Although Achebe portrays one sympathetic missionary character, the overriding focus of the book is on how the missionary encounter destroyed the integrity and solidarity of an Igbo village in precolonial Nigeria.

debates flourished in the 1960s and 1970s on whether there should be a "moratorium on the missions" to enable African Christians to find their own identities after decades of missionary paternalism and European co- lonial dominance.[2] And yet, for better and for worse, international mission remains alive and well in the twenty-first century, from the transnational Pentecostal movement to American students' affinity for short-term mis- sion trips in developing countries.[3] Tonino Pasolini and Sherry Meyer offer much insight on what it could mean to do fruitful—and not predatory— mission work in our own time.

FIGURE 8

Similar themes of missionary disruption leading to social violence are echoed in other popular novels on Africa, such as Barbara Kingsolver's *The Poisonwood Bible*.

2. This debate was admittedly more vociferous within mainline Protestantism than Catholicism. See Anderson, "Moratorium on Missionaries?"

3. Such mission work also continues to spark controversy, whether through overt proselytizing or through concerns that short-term missions do more harm than good in host countries. A case in point is that of Renée Bach, a 20-year-old American evangelical who set up a clinic in Jinja for malnourished children and was later accused of complicity in the deaths of dozens of Ugandan children. See Aizenman and Gharib, "American with No Medical Training."

In addition, mass media has become a primary form of mission in the modern world. Television channels like America's Evangelical Word Television Network (EWTN) and Canada's Salt and Light have become fixtures in the North American Catholic media landscape. In Uganda, the Catholic Church has a long history of spreading its social mission through the news media; its daily newspaper *Munno* was one of the most important news sources of any type in colonial and early post-colonial Africa.[4] Today, Catholics compete with their media-savvy Christian brethren to launch websites, podcasts, and social media platforms designed to capture the fickle attention of Millennials and Generation Z. Where Radio Pacis and its founders stand out, however, is in the way they are using radio as a means toward social transformation of the local community.

Before diving into the stories of Meyer and Pasolini, I will offer a bit of background on the Comboni tradition from which they emerged. The Comboni Missionaries of the Heart of Jesus took their name from St. Daniel Comboni, an Italian from the Verona region who was one of the first nineteenth-century Europeans to come to Africa as a member of the Mazza Institute. Nearly all the members of his party died on that first 1857 mission in Sudan, prompting some rethinking on the part of Comboni. In 1864, he conceived his "Plan for the Regeneration of Africa" after a long period of prayer at the tomb of St. Peter. In this plan, Comboni emphasized the need to "save Africa through Africa" through establishing institutes in Africa where local Christians could be trained as catechists, artisans, teachers, religious sisters, and seminarians.[5] Soon he formed a new missionary community to carry forward his vision, putting this under the strict control of the Holy See and Propaganda Fide. He later convinced the First Vatican Council to endorse a broader Church commitment to the central African missions. In 1873, Pope Pius IX named him as Pro-Vicar for Central Africa, although he would later be outflanked by Charles Lavigerie and the White Fathers in the region. Comboni spent much of the last decade of his life moving between Europe and Sudan; he died of a fever in Sudan in October 1881.[6]

4. On the history of Christian newspapers in Uganda, especially journalism's intersection with politics, see Sekeba, *Media Bullets in Uganda*.

5. In contrast to his famous Protestant contemporary David Livingstone, Comboni did not include in his plan "kings, presidents, emperors, [or] middle-class businessmen looking for profit" (Cisternino, *Passion for Africa*, 63).

6. Gilli, *Daniel Comboni*, 7–14.

Theologically, Comboni applied traditional Catholic devotion to the Sacred Heart of Jesus to evangelization, emphasizing that the "wellspring of mission" originated with the sacrificial love of Christ on the Cross.[7] Crucially, for Comboni, Christ had shed his blood for all human beings, and it was now the "hour of Africa"—the time for missionaries to bring the saving gospel message to the continent.[8] Not surprisingly, Comboni shared the paternalism of his era, describing Africans as "the most unfortunate race in the world" and lamenting the "deep distress of these poor people . . . who groan in the deep darkness of paganism."[9] His sense of the high physical and spiritual stakes involved in mission undergirded his famous motto, "Africa or Death!" His final recorded words captured this abiding sense of martyrdom. "I am happy in the Cross, which, when borne willingly out of love for God, gives birth to victory and eternal life."[10]

In 1910, thirty years after Comboni's death, the first Comboni missionaries entered West Nile province in northwestern Uganda. Comboni Missionary Sisters arrived eight years later. Together, the Comboni fathers and sisters went on to become the Catholic evangelists *par excellence* across the northern regions of West Nile, Acholiland, Lango, and Karamoja. They inculcated Catholic devotional practices such as Eucharistic adoration, the rosary, and the stations of the cross, and they also became renowned for their work in linguistics, carpentry, and medicine.[11] Politically, their legacy is mixed. Comboni wrote against British abuses in northern Uganda and Sudan in the early 1870s, yet later seemed to encourage a European colonial presence to ensure the future of the missions. By the 1950s, Comboni historians were describing the early British governor Samuel Baker as a Moses figure delivering the Acholi from pagan darkness to civilized light.[12] Yet their Italian and Catholic identities also made their situation tenuous in a British Anglican colony, leading to their internment and forced relocation during World Wars I and II. Several dozen more Combonis were expelled

---

7. Comboni's "plan for the regeneration of Africa" came during the canonization of St. Margaret Mary Alacoque, the seventeenth-century French mystic who initiated devotion to the Sacred Heart of Jesus (Whitmore, *Imitating Christ*, 56).

8. These insights were emphasized by Dada, "Comboni Day Lecture." See also Fernandez de Aller, "La Idea Misionera de Daniel Comboni," 265–80.

9. Gilli, *Daniel Comboni*, 74–75.

10. Gilli, *Daniel Comboni*, 236; Cisternino, *Passion for Africa*, 144.

11. On the history of Catholic missions in northern Uganda, see Cisternino, *Passion for Africa*, 340–490, and Pinkman, *Centenary of Faith*.

12. Whitmore, *Imitating Christ*, 64–67.

by the Obote and Amin regimes between 1967 and 1975 for their sociopolitical activism. Perhaps the most notable Comboni social activist was Fr. Tarcisio Agostoni, founder of *Leadership* magazine, godfather of Catholic social teaching in Uganda, and contributor to the rise of the Catholic-dominated Democratic Party in West Nile and Acholiland (chapter 1). Although Comboni numbers have declined with those of other European missionary congregations, they retain an important pastoral presence across northern Uganda. As of 2018, three of Uganda's bishops were Italian Combonis—the only non-Africans still serving in Uganda's episcopate. Among the few remaining European Comboni priests in West Nile is eighty-year-old Fr. Pasolini. It is to his story, and the intertwining story of the Comboni lay missionary Sherry Meyer, that we now turn.

The Missionary Journeys of Tonino Pasolini and Sherry Meyer

Born in 1939 in the northern Italian town of Cesena near Ravenna and Bologna, Tonino Pasolini's earliest memories involve running to caves to escape Allied bombing during World War II.[13] The oldest of five children, he grew up with a strong desire to be a priest and entered a diocesan minor seminary in 1950 at the age of eleven. He later moved to a major seminary in Bologna in 1955. His strong call to the priesthood was not matched, however, by a desire for missionary life. "I despised missionaries," he recounted, "for leaving Italy and not helping in their own home." He also shared many Italian diocesan clergy's condescending attitude that missionaries left Italy because they couldn't cut it as priests at home.

It took a sudden, Pauline call to change Tonino's attitude. "I remember the day and time distinctly. It was 4:00 p.m. on December 3, 1957."[14] Fr. Enrico Faré, a Comboni missionary based in Sudan, was visiting the Bologna seminary to recruit seminarians to respond to Pope Pius XII's call for priests to serve in Africa.[15] Faré's passion and strength of conviction left a lasting mark on the teenaged Pasolini. As he recalls, "God was calling me clearly, clearly." Significantly, for Tonino the call was more to Africa than

13. This biographical narrative, including quotations, is taken from Pasolini, interview, July 1–2, 2017. I also draw on more informal follow-up conversations with Fr. Pasolini at Radio Pacis in October 2018.

14. Coincidentally, December 3 is the feast day of St. Francis Xavier, the early modern Jesuit missionary to Asia and patron saint of Catholic missions.

15. See Pius XII, *Fidei Donum*.

missionary life *per se*; the Comboni missionary was expected to "give your soul, mind, energy, heart and body for Africa to bring the Good News to the people of Africa," focusing on "the most abandoned and neglected."[16]

It was the persistence of this "call to Africa" that sustained Pasolini after he began a novitiate with the Combonis in 1958. His parents opposed his decision to become a missionary, preferring that he stay closer to home in Italy. In turn, the Comboni formation house was marked by a stultifying conservatism that contrasted sharply with the more open atmosphere of his former seminary in Bologna. Tonino had a miserable experience as a Comboni novice; he lost forty-four pounds and developed ulcers within six months. "These were the worst two years of my life," he recalled. "If our mothers were to see us like this, they would have come and taken us home!" Yet ultimately his strong desire to go to Africa sustained him, and he was ordained a priest in 1964 during the Second Vatican Council. After the Council, he finally received his long-awaited call to the African missions, and he arrived in West Nile district in 1966.

As with his initial encounter with the Comboni seminary, Pasolini's adjustment to missionary life had its challenges. He asked the local Comboni parish priest about Lögbara culture and was told to learn how to eat cassava. "And remember," the priest added, "that they are an inferior race." In addition to missionaries' racist paternalism, Tonino arrived in a hostile political climate; Ugandan president Milton Obote expelled ten Comboni missionaries for alleged political interference in January 1967.[17] Sent to a new mission station, Tonino found a mentor in Fr. Sacco Luigi, a more progressive missionary committed to implementing the reform and renewal agenda of Vatican II. The Comboni General Chapter of 1969 also embraced the council and looked to renew the order by revitalizing Daniel Comboni's original focus on "the mission for Africa." Tonino found himself rediscovering the original call that had first carried him to the continent. Just as he was finding his feet, however, he was recalled to Italy in 1971 to direct postulants. In 1975, he was asked to lead the Combonis in Italy, becoming at age thirty-five the youngest Comboni provincial in the world.

In 1982, he stepped down from provincial leadership and returned to Uganda. After a brief stint in Karamoja, he came back to West Nile, where he settled in the town of Maracha near the Congolese border. Here

16. Pasolini, interview.

17. For more background on these incidents, see "Expulsion of Priests" and "'We're Innocent.'"

he channeled his energies into the formation of lay leaders and married couples. He also built a parish learning center to train catechists to work across Maracha's fifty-five substations, exhorting them to have "open eyes" so as to identify both the community's challenges and its emerging leaders. In 1990, Arua Bishop Frederick Drandua asked Pasolini to become the diocesan pastoral coordinator. Recognizing that he needed outside help, Tonino wrote to his contacts at the Volunteer Missionary Movement to request an English-speaking lay missionary with background in teaching, administration, and academic theology. As it turned out, VMM had only one candidate who fit this bill: Ms. Sherry Meyer.

Born in 1951, Sherry Meyer grew up about as far from Uganda as one can imagine—namely in a small suburb of Indianapolis, Indiana.[18] The oldest of six children, she attended Franciscan Catholic schools from primary school through university, becoming the first member of her family to graduate from college. Not only did she think that "all priests were Franciscans,"[19] but the Franciscans strongly shaped her understanding of Catholicism, inculcating in her values of simplicity and social justice. After graduation she worked as a high school English teacher. She quickly moved into administration. While still in her twenties, she was appointed as a high school principal at her alma mater. In the late 1980s, she went to work for the Archdiocese of Chicago. Here she felt a call to study theology and decided to pursue a graduate degree at Catholic Theological Union in Chicago. She assumed she would either keep working at the archdiocesan offices or go back to Indiana to work in parish ministry—until, that is, she started dreaming about Africa.

Far from embracing a romantic dream of missionary life, though, Meyer initially resisted this call. Questions churned in her head. How could she leave her close-knit family? What if she got sick? How could she stoop to begging friends and family for mission appeals after years of proudly supporting herself? And perhaps most of all, "What good can a forty-year-old American woman do in Africa?"[20] But over weeks and months of discernment, the call remained persistent, even as her family greeted the idea with what Meyer described as "much wailing and gnashing of teeth."

18. Biographical information is drawn from Meyer, interview, July 1–2, 2017. I also draw on more informal follow-up conversations with Ms. Meyer (Author's Field Notes, Radio Pacis, October 8–9, 2018).

19. Meyer, interview.

20. Meyer, interview.

Encouraged by friends and colleagues in Chicago, Meyer decided to join VMM, one of the only Catholic agencies dedicated exclusively to lay ministry and mission.

After several months of training in the UK, she made it to Uganda in October 1991, just in time for the Catholic Church's annual worldwide celebration of "Mission Sunday." Despite the apparent liturgical serendipity, the initial auguries were not good. Her roommate came down with hives; Sherry's asthma kicked in; she had no toilet for the first time in her life. "Every day I said, I can't do this, I am going home!"[21] She had to learn to be totally dependent on others, a mentality that did not come easily to an oldest child and single woman who had prized personal independence all her life. Now she found herself asking, "How do you take a bath here with a basin and soap? How do you hold a chicken? How do you prevent it from *^#$! on me?"[22]

Given these challenges, Meyer told herself she would complete a year of service and then go home to the US. But Fr. Tonino subtly worked on her. Recognizing her administrative abilities and passion for lay ministry, he invited her to help the Combonis develop a new lay-ministry training program. Realizing she could make a tangible contribution to the local church as a teacher and formator, Meyer developed a renewed sense of purpose that enabled her to grind through the daily deprivations of life in West Nile. Her overall mission was straightforward if not simple—to help local people realize that the Church was far more than priests and religious, and that laity were called to be "participants [in the Church] rather than spectators."[23] Her vision also matched Pasolini's and other Combonis' growing recognition that in the face of massive population growth and declining missionary numbers, the old model of house-to-house priest visits must give way to training and empowering lay leaders to evangelize each other.

Toward this end, Sherry was soon engaged in a variety of pastoral ministries, working out of the new *Christus Centre* that she and Tonino helped construct in Arua town in the early 1990s. Her ministries included teaching Scripture to lay catechists, running collaborative workshops for priests and laity, planning two diocesan synods, and translating the South African Lumko Institute's pastoral materials into local languages.[24] In fact,

---

21. Meyer, interview.

22. Meyer, interview.

23. Meyer, interview.

24. The South African Lumko Institute had a major impact on Catholic lay ministry

90 percent of the materials for Ugandan Catholic "liturgies in the absence of a priest"[25] were developed by Meyer, enabling catechists to share Sunday Eucharist with local Christians during the months or even years between priestly visits. Meyer realized she was also offering a unique image for the Ugandan church—a laywoman engaged in pastoral and liturgical ministry. Although some of the old-school Italian Comboni priests fretted that she was one of these "wild, American, feminist women who go to theology school,"[26] Sherry's deep faith and pastoral results slowly won them over. When her two-year contract with VMM ran out in the late 1990s, she affiliated with the Combonis as a lay missionary, attracted in part by the Combonis' "down home" attitudes that focused on what "needs to be done." Such practicality soon opened Sherry and Tonino to an innovative form of pastoral mission: taking the peace of Christ to the airwaves.

Gospel Values Radio: The Story of Radio Pacis

In 2001, representatives of the Diocese of Arua met with local Comboni missionaries to discuss how to evangelize via radio. Radio was the primary means of social communication in the region, and yet the Catholic Church had no presence on the local radio. Instead, the airwaves were dominated by stations owned by local politicians looking to make money and ensure votes come election time. Three recent diocesan synods had concluded that Catholic radio was a pressing pastoral need in a predominantly oral culture.[27] And yet Pasolini and Meyer hesitated, as they had no previous background in media or communications. As Pasolini confessed, "we didn't know anything about radio! But we loved the people."[28] Recognizing its pastoral importance, however, they agreed to spearhead the initiative. Between 2001 and 2004, they received extensive training from Austrian journalists and technicians on how to operate and sustain a successful radio station. Finally, in October 2004, Radio Pacis went on the air.

The station's name came on the suggestion of Bishop Drandua. "Radio Pacis" was chosen in part due to the local church's commitment to building intertribal and interreligious peace, especially in the midst of the northern

formation in Africa in the post-Vatican II era.

25. Meyer, interview.

26. Meyer, interview.

27. Idraku, interview.

28. Author's field notes, October 9, 2018.

region's history of conflict.[29] Yet the name also highlighted Radio Pacis's more holistic understanding of Catholic radio, distinguishing it from the exclusively devotional programming of other Ugandan Catholic stations such as Radio Maria. To be sure, Pasolini and Meyer ensured that the station broadcast Mass, liturgical music, catechesis, biblical reflection, and the rosary. For example, Meyer has aired a weekly "Scripture Moments" radio program for over a decade, and the radio offers catechetical programs on topics such as the meanings of the liturgical seasons.[30] In turn, Friday staff meetings begin with reflections on the upcoming Sunday gospel, and staff are invited to attend daily Mass at the station.[31] But Meyer and Pasolini also wanted the station to embody the social dimension of "gospel values," namely by addressing questions of human rights, health, education, sports, family, gender relations, and civic education. For Meyer, this focus on human lives echoes Jesus's own ministry. "Jesus always preferred the poor, the lame, the sick, and those on the margins, and this entails issues of justice, human rights, courts, corruption, and healthcare access."[32] Or as Radio Pacis production assistant Prudence Joan Onen put it, "People here believe that once you are poor, you are poor. The radio helps them to see how they can come out of their poverty and do things to improve their lives."[33]

Launched on October 25, 2004, Radio Pacis quickly became the most popular radio station in the region. Today it has a listenership estimated at 10 million, reaching villagers across northern Uganda, northeastern Congo, and South Sudan. This outreach is facilitated by the station's decision to broadcast in six languages—Acholi, Alur, Madi, Lögbara, Kakwa, and English. In turn, Radio Pacis has crossed more than just national and linguistic borders; their highest listening percentage is in the overwhelmingly

---

29. The home region of Idi Amin, West Nile suffered greatly during the post-Amin instability and civil war when government soldiers took revenge on many of Amin's former soldiers and local civilians. The Combonis stayed with the local people during this time, once famously intervening to halt a massacre of Muslims taking shelter at Ombaci Catholic parish. Comboni missionaries also accompanied West Nile residents when they fled into exile in Congo between 1981 and 1984 (Baltz and Pasolini, interview). Growing out of Alice Lakwena's Holy Spirit Movement, Joseph Kony's Lord's Resistance Army (LRA) rebellion—and the brutal government response—ravaged Acholiland and Lango districts between the late 1980s and the mid-2000s. This war rarely crossed the Nile River into West Nile district, however.

30. Meyer, interview.

31. Idraku, interview.

32. Meyer, interview.

33. Onen, interview, October 8, 2018.

Muslim district of Yumbe. Asked to explain the station's success outside the Catholic community, Meyer posited that local people of all religious stripes appreciate the station's commitment to "accuracy, truth, and balance" in a news media landscape dominated by politicization and bribery.[34] The station's popularity has helped it gain further support from local businesses. Through advertising, product sales, and fundraising, the station now raises more than 70 percent of its operating budget from local sources,[35] and at least twenty-two of their twenty-four hours of daily programming are locally produced.[36]

This local support reflects Radio Pacis's abiding strength as a socially engaged community radio station. Since 2010, the station has sponsored "community engagement" efforts in which field reporters move into villages to inquire into the felt needs of the community. Radio Pacis then hosts a forum in the village that enables ordinary people to voice their concerns directly to their civic leaders. Later, the radio station follows up to see if local leaders have kept their promises (the station's huge listenership provides ample motivation for the recalcitrant politician). In turn, Radio Pacis has focused on sensitizing the local population on questions of human dignity, such as child sexual abuse, alcoholism, and domestic violence.[37] According to Sarah Amviko, Radio Pacis's Human Resources manager, women are now speaking more openly about domestic violence. "[The radio] has empowered women to stand their ground and to know that they are human beings."[38] For Meyer, Radio Pacis's impact in this area was captured by comments she received from an older man in a local supermarket who thanked her for the attention the station pays to spousal relations. "The things you say on the radio are really unique—no one else can say that to us!" For Meyer, this demonstrates how radio can be akin to a social liturgy, creating a sacred space that facilitates an elevated conversation on questions of human dignity.[39]

A good example of this "elevated conversation" is provided by "We Go Forward," one of Radio Pacis's most popular morning programs. In a recent

34. Meyer, interview.

35. Avoku, interview.

36. Meyer, interview.

37. Aroga, interview.

38. Amviko, interview, October 10, 2018.

39. Meyer, interview.

focus group, residents praised the program for improving family life.[40] After listening to a program on domestic conflict, one local man foreswore physically abusing his wife in favor of nonviolent forms of conflict resolution. Still another woman in nearby Maracha District argued that "We Go Forward" lifted the self-esteem of such marginalized groups as women and children, people with disabilities and people living with HIV/AIDS. "Being a discordant couple [one partner is HIV positive and the other is not], I used to fear to disclose my status," she says. "But having listened to the program *Ama Mu Drile* ["We Go Forward"] on Radio Pacis, I freely came out to tell people about my status."[41]

As hundreds of thousands of South Sudanese refugees have poured into northern Uganda since 2014,[42] Radio Pacis has expanded this community outreach to engage refugee communities. They have kept refugee organizations accountable for their services, such as a recent exposé on the UNHCR's and World Food Program's problematic efforts to centralize food distribution.[43] Radio programs such as the Rural Initiative Community Empowerment (RICE) bring together refugees and local host communities to discuss areas of shared concern and conflict such as environmental destruction and infrastructural development. Other weekly programs like "Voice of the Voiceless" and "Refugee Hour" enable refugees to speak directly on their own situations.[44] For longtime reporter Gabriel Adrapi, this reflects Radio Pacis's mission that "whatever we do, we do for the voiceless of the community."[45]

Radio Pacis also strives to practice what it preaches through its training and apprenticing of staff. Many RP staff have come through the radio's "Candidate Mentor Program," a competitive four-week apprenticeship that has provided more professional staff for radio stations across Uganda.[46] Recently, delegations from stations in South Sudan and Malawi have

---

40. Radio Pacis, "Assessing the Impact," 2.

41. Radio Pacis, "Assessing the Impact," 2.

42. The South Sudan civil war broke out in December 2013 between ethno-military factions associated with South Sudan's president, Salva Kiir (a Dinka), and the country's Vice-President, Riek Machar (a Nuer). The conflict has killed nearly 400,000 people, nearly matching the death toll in Syria (O'Grady, "New Report"). On the history of South Sudan and its recent conflicts, see Johnson, *South Sudan*.

43. Adrapi, interview.

44. Atule, interview.

45. Adrapi, interview.

46. Adrapi, interview; Atule, interview; Ayikobua, interview.

come for training.[47] In turn, RP managers have apprenticed with the best mass-media agencies in the field, including BBC World Service, Uganda Media Development Foundation, Farm Radio International, the Konrad Adenauer Foundation, and Radio Vatican.[48] The radio station also looks to build self-sufficiency among staff, for example through instituting a jointly owned goat farm as a financial source for micro-loans and salary supplements.[49] In addition, Meyer and Pasolini refused early pressure to hire only Catholics, basing their hiring choices rather on merit; Protestants and Muslims serve in prominent management positions at the station. For Pasolini, this interreligious hiring reflects West Nile residents' general interreligious harmony: "We live together! We plan together! We stay together! This is the real Uganda!"[50]

In turn, multiple staff members spoke of how much they appreciate Meyer's and Pasolini's consultative leadership style, including a tradition of weekly Friday meetings where staff are given free rein to share praises and raise critiques in small groups and free-flowing roundtable discussions.[51] When asked to explain the station's success, Station Manager Gaetano Apamaku highlighted the "decentralization" of Radio Pacis, noting that "in leadership you have to trust other people to do things."[52] For program manager Noel Ayikobua, "they [Sherry and Tonino] involve everyone in decision-making."[53] In the view of Assistant Director Fr. Charles Idraku, Meyer and Pasolini are willing to correct people but don't hold grudges, and the overall atmosphere is one of encouragement; there is not a "director zone" dividing the leadership from the rest of the staff.[54] For Human Resources director Sarah Amviko, the ultimate measure of Meyer, Pasolini, and Radio Pacis is maturation rather than market share. "Radio Pacis has

47. Apamaku, email communication.

48. Apamaku, interview.

49. If there was one consistent internal critique of Radio Pacis among staff members, it was the station's low salaries. This was also cited as the primary reason for staff turnover (Author's field notes, October 8, 2018).

50. Pasolini, interview.

51. Onen, interview; Adrapi, interview; Author's field notes, May 24, 2019.

52. Apamaku, interview.

53. Ayikobua, interview.

54. Idraku, interview.

not just inspired people but made people grow . . . As a human being, what can I do to be a better person?"[55]

Lessons in Leadership for the Postcolonial Missionary

In terms of broader lessons in Catholic leadership, what can we learn from Radio Pacis and the postcolonial missionary witness of Fr. Tonino Pasolini and Sherry Meyer? First, the radio station itself offers a powerful witness to the value of bridging the Church's devotional and social missions. Too often in the Western context, the Church finds itself divided between a justice-oriented "liberal" wing that emphasizes the Church's social teachings and a devotional "conservative" wing that emphasizes liturgical and prayer practices. Radio Pacis embodies an invaluable Catholic "both-and" position on this question. West Nile Catholics tune in to Radio Pacis to hear Mass, say the rosary, learn about the Bible, and gain insight on Church teachings and liturgical seasons. Yet they also listen to learn about how women should be treated in the home and to challenge political leaders to deliver on promised infrastructure.

Second, Meyer, Pasolini, and the Combonis remind us that the missionary's greatest gift remains his or her long-term presence in solidarity with the people. In Meyer's words, "the difference between missionaries and development workers is that missionaries come to stay and live."[56] For Pasolini, long-term presence enables a missionary to learn what is really needed within a community and provides sufficient time to implement and evaluate a pastoral initiative.[57] And although he recognizes the value of all of the Combonis' pastoral projects, Pasolini argues that the Comboni legacy cannot be encompassed by the radio stations, health centers, wells, and churches that stretch across northern Uganda. "The people will not remember what we've done. But they will remember the way that we've stayed with them."[58] The Combonis have paid a price for their solidarity. Fifteen Comboni missionaries have suffered violent deaths in Uganda since 1975,[59] and Pasolini himself was nearly killed by the LRA in 1997 as he

55. Amviko, interview, July 3, 2017.

56. Meyer, interview.

57. "It [pastoral work] takes time to bear fruit. It can't happen in one or two years." (Pasolini, interview).

58. Pasolini, interview.

59. Baltz and Pasolini, interview. Most of these deaths happened in northern Uganda,

traveled in a bus convoy back to Arua. In this sense, the Combonis reflect the incarnational risk of Christianity, a religion that proclaims a Son of God who emptied himself, took the form of a slave, and offered his life for the community (Phil 2:6–8). Or as Fr. Tonino puts it, "the final witness of the Comboni is not words but life."[60]

Third, Meyer and Pasolini embrace a missiology best captured in John the Baptist's words at the beginning of John's Gospel: "He must increase, and I must decrease" (John 3:30). In this vein, Meyer describes her ministry as one of "empowering the people," and Pasolini argues that missionaries must "prepare the way for others."[61] Such an approach entails moving away from the spirit of paternalism that marked so much of the colonial missionary project in Uganda, recognizing that God was in Africa long before Christian missionaries arrived—and that God will be here long after they depart. And whereas locals tended to see colonial missionaries as "people who give things," breeding dependency, the postcolonial missionary must train laity to evangelize each other.[62] Pasolini describes this commitment in terms of the Lögbara proverb, *ocema ceni*, or "self-reliance." "The hoe is a symbol of our faith," he says. "We need to develop fields where the community grows things. If we work for our community, we have understood what it means to be Christian."[63] The Combonis have generally practiced what they preach; today only two parishes remain in Comboni hands in West Nile. In this regard, Meyer, Pasolini, and the Combonis offer an important witness for both the African political leaders and NGOs who often struggle to put themselves out of business.

Fourth, Radio Pacis witnesses to the importance of effective management and organization. When asked about her own legacy, Meyer does not invoke language of transformation. Rather, she speaks of "competence," "organization," and "planning."[64] Pasolini and Meyer note that any success-

but Comboni missionaries also suffered in other parts of the country. A longtime lay catechist recounted to me the 1981 martyrdom of Italian Comboni Fulvio Christoforetti, shot for speaking out against government repression in the Luwero district of south-central Uganda (Ndarhuka, interview).

60. Pasolini, "Homily for Daniel Comboni Day."

61. Meyer, interview; Pasolini, interview.

62. Idraku, interview.

63. Pasolini, interview. Or as American Comboni David Baltz puts it, "our role is to plant the church and let it grow, not to run things forever" (Baltz, interview).

64. Meyer, interview. Meyer later joked that when asked what she does in Africa, she responds, "I teach employment!" (Author's field notes, October 9, 2018).

ful Catholic organization must be true to its mission, able to provide ample motivation, and marked by strong management.[65] It is important to note that the "three Ms" here do not include the word "messiah." All leaders have weaknesses, and they surround themselves with others who, in Meyer's words, "compensate for our liabilities."[66] As Charles Idraku puts it, "This place shows that something can be done the right way. . . . It is a matter of making a working system, of having policies, of having a team that believes in what they are doing."[67] In contrast to Sr. Rose Muyinza's Daughters of Charity, Radio Pacis demonstrates that creative charisma must be balanced by effective institutional organization. In Meyer's words, "My legacy is administration; Catholics tend to thrive in building institutions. But many institutions in Africa are failing because of failures in management and administration."[68]

In this regard, a final important leadership lesson concerns Radio Pacis's commitment to quality and excellence. Sherry and Tonino lacked experience in radio, but they sought out Austrian trainers who could teach them best practices. They have sent their staff to train with the best international organizations in radio. This investment in training enabled field reporter Gabriel Adrapu to win a national reporting award after only two years on the job.[69] Most famously, Radio Pacis won BBC Radio's inaugural "Best New Radio Station in Africa" award in 2007. The award validated Pasolini's and Meyer's meritocratic vision. In Pasolini's words, "If I put my energy, mind, and heart in something, I want this to be the best."[70] This ethos of excellence continues to shape Radio Pacis's culture over a decade after the BBC award. In the words of Tonny Ayoku, the station's public relations and sales manager, "At Radio Pacis, they [Sherry and Tonino] have

---

65. Author's field notes, October 9. 2018.

66. Meyer, interview.

67. Idraku, interview. Radio Pacis's current Human Resources Manager, Sarah Amviko, also emphasized the comparative formality of Radio Pacis's HR approach in terms of personnel policies, formal one-year contracts, and offering clear job expectations to new employees (Amviko, interview, October 10, 2018).

68. Meyer, interview.

69. Adrapu, interview.

70. Pasolini, interview. In 2014, the station was also honored with a European Union award for its pioneering work with solar panels. Radio Pacis is now off the local electricity grid and producing enough solar energy on a sunny day to supply all of Arua town's power needs. This enables the station to be on the air twenty-four hours a day and seven days a week, which is no mean feat in electricity-challenged Uganda (Author's field notes, October 8, 2018).

taught us to strive for the best. They inculcate this attitude in everyone. You don't settle for less. You always do your best."[71]

Like "ambassadors for Christ" (2 Cor 5:19), Sherry Meyer and Tonino Pasolini continue to move between worlds, even as they soldier on in their beloved West Nile. They each spend several months a year back home in Italy and the United States, fundraising and reconnecting with family. Fr. Tonino is in the process of handing over directorship of Radio Pacis to Fr. Idraku. Pasolini is also returning to his missionary roots in pastoral care; the local bishop recently appointed him as pastor of St. Martha Parish in Katrini, a new parish in Pasolini's old stomping grounds in the Maracha area. Now in her late sixties and nearly thirty years into what was initially a two-year volunteer contract, Meyer also remains actively engaged with both the radio station and the local church. In November 2018, she helped coordinate the Diocese of Arua's fifth diocesan synod on the theme of "family." Their long-term commitment does not go unnoticed. In the words of local Comboni priest Fr. Romanus Dada, "We are proud of them. I appreciate them so much. They have given their lives to this place. We hope they die here!"[72]

Reflection Questions

1. Should Western missionaries still evangelize in Africa? Should African missionaries evangelize in the West? If not, why not? If so, why and how?

2. What would be the ideal traits for a student volunteer doing mission, service, or justice work in a foreign country?

3. If you were designing a Catholic radio station, what would the twenty-four-hour schedule look like?

4. How could Catholic media contribute to social justice in your local context?

71. Ayoku, interview.
72. Dada, interview.

6

Mama Peace

Rosalba Ato Oywa

ON A WARM MORNING in November 2018 at the beginning of Gulu's dry season, I came to visit with Rwot Latim Baptist. The chief of the influential Pawel clan in Acholiland, Rwot Latim looked the part, exuding a calm sense of self-assurance and towering over me as we walked up to his compound in a small village outside Gulu town. The chairman of the board of People's Voice for Peace (PVP), a local NGO, he smiled broadly as he reflected on the reason for our meeting. "Ahh, you are here to talk about Mama Peace! She is not just a mother to her children, but to all of Acholiland!"[1]

It is to Mrs. Rosalba Ato Oywa—aka "Mama Peace"—that we now turn as the final profile of Ugandan Catholic leadership in this book. Overshadowed internationally by figures such as Archbishop John Baptist Odama, Sr. Rosemary Nyirumbe, and Mrs. Angelina Atyam, Rosalba Oywa is renowned locally for over thirty years of commitment to analyzing and engaging the root causes of northern Uganda's conflicts. Like so many in the region, she herself suffered greatly in the war that subsumed the north between 1986 and 2008, losing family members, her home, and nearly her own life. Rather than remain a passive victim, she turned her suffering into a lifelong pursuit of truth, justice, and reconstruction for and with the men, women, and children of Acholiland. Nominated with 1,000 other global

---

1. Baptist, interview.

FIGURE 9

women's activists for a collective 2005 Nobel Peace Prize,[2] Oywa reminds us of the importance of social analysis in the task of peacebuilding. As a Catholic laywoman who has made her primary impact in civil society, Rosalba also offers a model of public leadership notable for its amplification of local voices, unflinching commitment to truth, and long-term accompaniment of her people.

As indicated by the renowned work of Catholic leaders such as Odama, Atyam, and Nyirumbe, however, Oywa's peace witness has not unfolded in a vacuum. Before turning to her life and work, let us first contextualize her contribution within the extensive peacebuilding work of the Catholic Church in northern Uganda.

2. "Rosalba Ato Oywa."

Multisectoral Catholic Peacebuilding in Northern Uganda

*"Peacebuilding is like the work of the earthworms. Let us collaborate
and build on all other initiatives by different stakeholders."* —Rosalba Oywa and George Omona, 2001[3]

In his 2005 book *From Crisis to Kairos: The Mission of the Church in the Time
of HIV/AIDS, Refugees, and Poverty,* Jesuit theologian Agbonkhianmeghe
Orobator sketches a vision of what he calls the "multisectoral church." In
essence, the multisectoral church is a church that collaborates with other
civil society and state actors to solve a shared social problem in service to
the common good. In Orobator's words, "the church cannot 'go it alone,'
and [this] imposes on it the imperative of recognizing God's action in all
spheres of human endeavor, and cooperating with other religious (Christian and non-Christian) and secular bodies."[4] Likewise, the multisectoral
approach entails seeing the church as a "multifaceted sector," a "mosaic"
of local actors that collectively comprise the community of faith's response
to a broad social challenge. Orobator sees this "multisectoral" approach as
the primary way in which the Ugandan church approached the HIV-AIDS
crisis in the 1990s. The same could be said for the Catholic Church's multifaceted involvement in peacebuilding in northern Uganda over the past
quarter-century.

First, Catholic leaders such as Archbishop John-Baptist Odama have
collaborated with other religious leaders to advocate for peace in the region. The most famous of these efforts is the Acholi Religious Leaders Peace
Initiative (ARLPI), founded in 1998 to present a united religious voice for
peace among Catholics, Muslims, Anglicans, Orthodox, and later Seventh-
Day Adventists and Born-Again Pentecostals. In the face of a "conflict that
did not discriminate based on faith," Odama, Anglican Bishop Mackleod
Baker Ochola, and Muslim Sheikh Musa Khelil realized that they needed
to "come up with a joint voice and work together" to place more pressure
on the NRM government and the LRA to negotiate.[5] The ARLPI began as
a venue for interreligious prayers in Gulu, Lira, and Kitgum, and quickly
grew into a broader mediation effort between the NRM government and
the LRA. Over the next decade, the ARPLI kept open dialogue channels
and consistently advocated for a restorative rather than retributive solution

3. Omona and Oywa, "Plight of Children in Conflict," 4.

4. Orobator, *From Crisis to Kairos,* 125.

5. Khelil, interview.

to northern Uganda's war.[6] For his part, Odama became the closest thing to an international household name from Catholic Uganda, renowned for his mediation work and his solidarity with child "night walkers" in Gulu town.[7]

The Catholic Church's commitment to dialogue was also embodied in the "Peace Weeks" that Archbishop Odama started in 2006. Although initiated in Gulu Archdiocese, these events gathered Catholic representatives from surrounding dioceses in Arua, Nebbi, and Lira in order to build trust across various tribal and clan lines, adopting the acronym of GANAL— "Grow All New Alive in Love."[8] In particular, Archbishop Odama—himself an ethnic Lögbara from neighboring West Nile district—wanted surrounding communities to realize the Acholi were not solely responsible for the killing and had in fact suffered disproportionate violence at the hands of the LRA.[9] Organized around different themes each year, Peace Week offers extended time for reflection, prayer, and social analysis of the root causes of conflict and key priorities in post-war reconstruction. In addition to providing a space where northerners can "share their bitterness" from the war,[10] Peace Week creates opportunities for participants to apologize and seek forgiveness on behalf of their compatriots, such as when the Sudanese bishop of Torit apologized on behalf of his country's contributions to the war.[11] In recent years, the Peace Week tradition has expanded to include "Dialogue Caravans" in which Catholic leaders travel to villages to seek local residents' input on the long-term challenges of reconstruction.[12] These annual efforts are complemented by Catholic radio stations such as Lira's Radio Wa. During the war, Radio Wa called rebels out of the bush, and the station now airs a weekly "Visions for Peace" program, reflecting the station's beatitudinal motto, "Blessed are the Peacemakers."[13]

6. On the broader story of the ARPRI and the war, see Hoekema, *We Are the Voice of the Grass,* and Hoekema, "Risking Peace."

7. On the spiritual vision that underlay Odama's public advocacy, see Katongole, *Journey of Reconciliation,* 121–36.

8. The motto reflected the acronym of the founding dioceses: Gulu Archdiocese, Nebbi Diocese, Arua Diocese, and Lira Diocese. Opongo, "At the Frontlines," 68.

9. Since LRA founder Joseph Kony was an ethnic Acholi, other tribal groups tended to collectively blame the Acholi for the war and LRA atrocities.

10. Oywa, interview, November 26, 2018.

11. Oywa, interview, July 17, 2017; Ocen P'akec, interview.

12. Okot, interview.

13. Otonga, interview.

The Catholic Church in northern Uganda has also been extensively involved in social reconstruction. The Church's official development arm, Caritas, provides social services, constructs schools and dispensaries, enhances food security through training in sustainable farming, and facilitates economic empowerment through job training. In Gulu district, two-thirds of Caritas beneficiaries are women.[14] These vocational training initiatives have also unfolded in less centralized ways. Notable efforts here include Sr. Rosemary Nyirumbe's St. Monica's Vocational School in Gulu, offering training in catering, sewing, and other fields for young women returning from the war,[15] and Quilinous Otim's Ave Maria Vocational Training and Youth Development Center in Lira, providing job-skills training in fields such as dressmaking, carpentry, mechanics, and subsistence farming.[16]

The Catholic Church has also contributed to perhaps the most important form of post-conflict reconstruction: the healing of minds and souls. For all of its physical destruction, the war's deepest scars are unseen, namely the way "people are wounded deep inside their hearts."[17] This type of psychosocial rehabilitation takes much longer than physical reconstruction, and it does not necessarily draw international attention or donor funds. In the words of Steven Balmoi, a Catholic radio host for Gulu's Mega-FM, "People can remove a bullet, but no one gives a damn what you think."[18] Psychosocial counseling is thus one of the pressing ministerial priorities of Caritas and other Catholic organizations in northern Uganda.[19]

Through its Justice and Peace Commissions, the Catholic Church in northern Uganda is also addressing one of the single biggest ongoing disputes in post-war northern Uganda: land conflict. Upwards of 80 percent of the local population was displaced from their land at the height of the war, and more than 1.5 million residents of eastern and northern Uganda

14. Komakech Aludi, interview.

15. Sr. Rosemary has received much international acclaim for her work, including being named by *Time Magazine* as one of the 100 most influential people in the world in 2014. On the spiritual vision that undergirds her humanitarian work, see Katongole, *Born from Lament*, 134–42.

16. Otim, interview. Since its founding in 1984, Ave Maria has provided vocational training to 13,000 youth and young adults, including hundreds of refugees from South Sudan in recent years.

17. Ogwal, interview. A member of the Concerned Parents' Association of Lira, Ogwal had a daughter kidnapped by the LRA in 1996.

18. Balmoi, interview.

19. Komakech Aludi, interview.

were living in IDP camps in 2005.[20] In communities in which land was traditionally held in common, perhaps 90 percent of the local population lacked titles or legal claims to their land, and property boundaries were often ambiguous.[21] In recent years, investors affiliated with the Ugandan government and military have engaged in extensive land-grabbing in the north. In response to local land disputes, diocesan and parish-based Justice and Peace Commissions have trained local chiefs in mediation and conducted intra-family mediation efforts, often concluding these efforts with traditional reconciliation rituals such as *Mato Oput*.[22] In the context of higher-level investor land disputes, the Church has arranged public dialogues bringing families together with government stakeholders and religious and cultural leaders.

Finally, one should not overlook the Church's commitment to prayer. Both the ARLPI and the diocesan Peace Weeks were born in communal prayer. As Todd Whitmore has shown, deep personal devotion to the Eucharist, the rosary, and sacramental objects sustained the courageous social witness of religious communities like the Little Sisters of Mary Immaculate in Gulu.[23] Likewise, renowned lay groups such as the Concerned Parents Association—founded by a group of Catholic parents after their daughters were abducted in 1996 by the LRA—committed themselves to a discipline of *novena* prayers and regular fasting until their "Aboke girls" came back from the bush.[24] In response to the idolatrous theology of an LRA officially committed to the "Ten Commandments," these CPA parents implored the "real God" to intervene on their behalf and promised to "pray until God responded."[25] Not surprisingly, Uganda's growing Catholic Charismatic Movement has become a crucial part of the Church's integration of spiritual and physical healing for victims and perpetrators alike, especially in battling alcoholism.[26]

20. Allen and Vlassenroot, *Lord's Resistance Army*, viii.

21. Yasinto, interview.

22. Impressively, the Archdiocese of Gulu has Justice and Peace Commissions in all twenty-seven parishes. Later in this chapter, I will discuss the traditional Acholi restorative justice mechanism of *Mato Oput* in more depth.

23. Whitmore, *Imitating Christ*, 97–98, 105, 114.

24. See Acan, *Not Yet Sunset*, and De Temmeran, *Aboke Girls*.

25. Ogwal, interview.

26. Ogwal, interview.

In its official efforts to propagate ecumenical peacemaking, social re-construction, counseling, land conflict resolution, and prayer, the Catholic Church has been a "multisectoral" actor for peace in a region in which 70 percent of the population claims the Catholic faith.[27] One should not overly idealize the Church's efforts. For example, ecumenical dialogue has been much stronger at the elite level than at the grassroots, where the Christian churches have reached a modicum of coexistence if not conviviality.[28] In addition, southern Ugandan Catholics often lacked any sense of solidarity with their northern brothers and sisters during the LRA war, in part due to the abuses southerners suffered at the hands of the northern-dominated army in the 1970s and early 1980s.[29] Finally, the Church's Small Christian Communities (SCCs) have not been mobilized for peacemaking in the same way as their counterparts in, for example, the Democratic Republic of the Congo.[30]

But as she herself insisted to me on several occasions, Rosalba Oywa's notable peacebuilding leadership did not happen in isolation from the Catholic Church's broader efforts. As we will see, what is notable about Oywa as a Catholic leader is the extent to which she made her impact outside church institutions, embodying Vatican II's teaching that the pri-mary mission for lay Catholics is to "contribute to the sanctification of the world."[31] It is to Rosalba's witness as a Catholic leader in the public square that we now turn.

Agitator for Peace: The Life and Work of Rosalba Ato Oywa

Born in the village of Anaka in Gulu district, Rosalba Ato was the young-est daughter of six children. As a girl, she received a rare opportunity to pursue further education when her father became frustrated with her older brother's poor performance in school. Recognizing Rosalba's intellectual

27. Alava, "There is Confusion," 51.

28. On the competitive interactions of Protestant and Catholic churches in the re-gion, see Alava, "There is Confusion."

29. This came home to me at the 2004 Uganda Martyrs Day in Kampala when I saw numerous signs calling for southerners to wake up to the sufferings of their brothers and sisters in the north.

30. This critique was offered by Catholic Acholi chief Rwot Latim Baptist (Baptist, interview), but it also echoes my own conclusions after conducting comparative field-work on sample SCCs in DRC and Uganda (Carney, "People Bonded Together by Love").

31. Second Vatican Council, *Lumen Gentium*, 31.

aptitude, he informed his family, "Let my daughter go [to school]."[32] Rosalba proceeded to study at local Comboni schools in the Gulu area before receiving a scholarship to attend Mount St. Mary's Namagunga, one of Uganda's best Catholic girls' secondary schools near Kampala.[33] After secondary school, she finished a bachelor's degree in chemistry and biology at Makerere University, graduating in 1977 only months after her uncle, the government minister Erinayo W. Oryema, was assassinated along with the Acholi Anglican Archbishop Janani Luwum.[34] After graduation, she took a job as a secondary science teacher, married, and gave birth to three children.

Shortly after Museveni took power in 1986, and in response to harsh NRA counterinsurgency operations in the north, the Acholi prophetess Alice Lakwena sparked what was described as an "uprising of the Holy Spirit" against the NRA government. This provided the initial foundation for the better-known LRA movement led by Joseph Kony.[35] One of the first battles of the war broke out near Rosalba's school in Pabbo in August 1986. The headmaster was killed, and Oywa fled for her life. In the process, she lost her home and all of her possessions. "The only thing I could carry was my children and myself and the clothes we were wearing."[36] She and her children journeyed on foot for fifty kilometers to her husband's home village. Oywa describes this personal displacement as the foundation of her later activism. "It was just an experience that impacted so much on me. It shaped my life completely."[37] Her husband's brother, a Catholic priest, gave her family a place to live at Lachor Seminary, but the war caught up to her again. After two more years on the run, she settled in Gulu town in 1988. Rosalba's story reminds us that Christian activists do not necessarily choose to relocate to the margins; sometimes the margins come to them.

Rosalba Oywa's experience of deprivation, combined with her recognition of the limited opportunities for uneducated women to restart their

32. Oywa, interview, November 26, 2018.

33. Coincidentally, this school was also the alma mater of Sr. Rose Muyinza (see chapter 4).

34. Oywa, interview, November 26, 2018. Oyrema had been inspector general of police and later a cabinet minister in Amin's government, but Amin killed him due to suspicions that he was involved in an Acholi coup plot.

35. On the roots and development of the LRA conflict, see Behrend, *Alice Lakwena*, and Allen and Vlassenroot, *Lord's Resistance Army*.

36. Oywa, interview, July 17, 2017.

37. Oywa, interview, July 17, 2017.

lives, led her directly into advocacy work within the local community and the church. "When I saw ordinary women, just going through the same process like me, and without any support, without anything, then that itself motivated me to begin doing something toward either ending that war, or doing something that so many people don't continue suffering . . . From that time, I never looked back."[38] As a volunteer activist, she mobilized women in the community to stand up to the war and actively work for peace. In 1989, she and the Gulu Women's Development Committee organized a city-wide women's protest. Wearing rugs, singing funeral songs, and baring their breasts, women shut down the local market and marched through town demanding an end to the war. For a time, peace and stability were restored in the city and its environs.[39] Oywa was also a key instigator in pushing the Catholic Church into a more visible peacemaking role. In 1992, Oywa collaborated with the Archdiocese of Gulu to start an annual "March for Peace" in Gulu town. In 2006 she worked with Archbishop Odama and other archdiocesan officials to initiate the aforementioned Peace Week tradition. Three years later, she served as the chair of the 2009 Peace Week's central organizing committee.[40]

In 1988, she also made the decision to switch careers, leaving her job as a secondary science teacher to take up a position as a social analyst for the UK-based Agency for Cooperation for Research and Development (ACORD). As a "broad-based international consortium of non-government organizations" that is "independent of political and religious affiliations," ACORD coordinated field teams in sixteen African countries in the mid-1990s, focusing on questions of community marginalization, gender equality, and conflict transformation.[41] ACORD was the only international NGO to stay in northern Uganda through the worst years of the war in the 1990s. In her work with ACORD, Oywa looked beyond the headlines to examine the root causes of the conflict, such as the destabilizing impact of the collapse of the cotton market and cattle herds on men's economic security and gender relations. As she wrote in one 1994 document, "Men

38. Oywa, interview, July 17, 2017.

39. Oywa, "International Conference," 2; Oywa, interview, July 17, 2017; Tinkasiimire, "Women, Peacebuilding and Reconciliation," 73. This is similar to practices used by women during Liberia's civil war (see Gbowee, *Mighty Be Our Powers*, and Reticker, *Pray the Devil*).

40. Oywa, interview, July 17, 2017; Komakech Aludi, interview.

41. "Confidential ACORD-GULU," 10. For more information on ACORD's mission, history, and current activities, see their website, http://www.acordinternational.org.

are finding it hard to re-establish their place in post-war society, undermined by the loss of their cattle and the absence of off-farm employment; and social expectations as well as legal rights as regards land, marriage, and women's role are in a state of flux."[42] Rosalba also worked to build what she termed "participatory self-reliance" in the local community, whereby "affected people are assisted to gain knowledge and critically analyse their situation to identify local strategies and skills already in existence and suggest options required to solve the identified problems."[43]

Working through ACORD, Oywa headed up an all-women research team that documented ordinary women's testimonies during the early years of the war (1986–1994). She did this in part because she did not want to be an extractive researcher, drawing information out of local people without working with them, giving them hope, and collaborating with them to transform their situation.[44] These testimonies also enabled ordinary women's voices to be broadcast to an international audience. Emblematic here was the voice of "Edisa," a single mother speaking of her struggle to keep alive nineteen children in the midst of LRA kidnappings and the HIV-AIDS pandemic spreading through northern Uganda's IDP camps. "You have to nurse and bury your children one by one until you are left with nothing. You wish you never gave life."[45]

Building from her ACORD work documenting women's testimonies during the war, Rosalba founded the nonprofit group "People's Voices for Peace" in 1995. PVP was initially started to provide a voice for rural Acholi women, especially regarding issues of micro-credit loans, sexual and domestic violence, and the sidelining of women in the government's rehabilitation and development programs.[46] Yet by training and involving local women in the research, PVP also engaged in "participatory research" with local women, giving them a "deeper understanding of the nature, pattern, and dynamics of the armed conflict" that allowed them to directly engage key stakeholders.[47] Rosalba and PVP also reached out to local men,

---

42. Oywa, "PANOS—Uganda Briefing," 92. Alava notes that in the late 1980s, Acholi cattle herds declined from more than 120,000 to the single thousands, largely due to government-sponsored cattle raids (Alava, "There is Confusion," 148).

43. "Confidential ACORD-Gulu," 11.

44. Oywa, interview, July 17, 2017; Oywa, interview, November 26, 2018.

45. Quoted in Oywa, "PANOS—Uganda Briefing," 94.

46. Uganda Women's Network (UWONET) and People's Voice for Peace (PVP), "Report on Situation of Women," 1.

47. Oywa, "International Conference," 4.

recognizing that the challenges facing women and children could not be separated from those facing men. In the words of one PVP report,

> As a result of the various humiliations men have undergone and the increased levels of unemployment, many have resorted to heavy drinking and subsequently turned violent to their spouses. Much as UWONET's and PVP's focus is targeting women, there is need to devise gender-oriented action to help the men overcome their own vulnerability and cope with the effects of war.[48]

PVP also networked with over seventy local organizations working for peace and reconstruction in northern Uganda.[49]

From 1996, Oywa worked with a team of researchers to document both LRA and government abuses in the IDP camps established in the region. Euphemistically named "protected villages," the camps were more akin to "a death trap for the people."[50] In a hard-hitting 1997 report, Oywa and her all-women research team revealed the extensive sexual violence and physical mutilation practiced by the LRA. Yet they also lambasted the NRM government for its policy of "alienation, segregation and marginalization against the people of the North," including military operations carried out at harvest time that appeared to be "a strategy to starve people to death."[51] By the end of the 1990s, 80 percent of Gulu's population and 50 percent of the overall regional population were living in IDP camps,[52] and thousands were dying from atrocious camp conditions. Inflamed at Oywa's and ACORD's public reporting, local NRM politicians and military commanders tried to link her to the LRA rebels, and she began receiving death threats. In 2001, she told Human Rights Watch that she "was not safe," and friends urged her to leave the country.[53] At the end of the day, however, Rosalba could not bring herself to leave her suffering people. Even after ACORD asked its staff to relocate to Kampala, she stayed in Gulu, and she and PVP continued to document government torture throughout the early 2000s.[54] For her part, Oywa attributes her ultimate survival to divine

48. UWONET and PVP, "Report on Situation of Women," 2.

49. Oywa, interview, November 26, 2018.

50. Oywa, interview, July 17, 2017. Allen and Vlassenroot describe these as "rural prisons" (*Lord's Resistance Army*, 15).

51. "Confidential ACORD-Gulu," 13–14.

52. Maletta, *Gulu*, 30:40; Oywa, "Some of the Challenges," 1.

53. Oywa, interview, September 25, 2018.

54. See here Oywa and People's Voice for Peace, "Human Rights Monitoring."

agency. "We were working for the truth . . . It was now God who intervened, and we put all our hopes in prayer. I think God worked a miracle."[55]

In the 1990s, Oywa was also one of the key instigators in the revival of the traditional Acholi reconciliation practice of *Mato Oput*. In *Mato Oput*, a perpetrator must admit responsibility, seek forgiveness, and agree to pay compensation in cows or money to the victim's family. If the victim's family accepts this offer, the families come together for a day of celebratory feasting. Here families drink a bitter juice from the local *oput* tree, which symbolizes the purgative dimensions of reconciliation. Families then bend their spears "in a pledge to never turn their weapons against each other." According to local tradition, the spirit of the dead person is now appeased and will no longer haunt the perpetrator's family.[56] Oywa began studying the process of *Mato Oput* in 1988. A decade later, she narrated a case in the documentary film *Gulu: The Struggle for Peace*. Finally, in the year 2000, she lobbied the Belgian government to fund the revitalization and expansion of this reconciliation process.[57] Since then, *Mato Oput* has played a key role in restorative-justice initiatives in Acholiland.[58]

By the mid-2000s, prospects for peace were improving in the war-fatigued north. Oywa and her fellow women's activists did not leave anything to chance, however. During the 2006–2008 Juba peace talks that ultimately ushered in a lasting armistice, Oywa and other NGO leaders founded the "Women's Coalition for Peace," organized activists in a caravan to travel to South Sudan, and rallied outside the negotiation rooms to pressure both sides to come to terms.[59]

Although Joseph Kony did not sign the accords, Juba ultimately signaled the unofficial end of the war in the north. Oywa remained integrally involved in post-war reconstruction.[60] In 2009, she worked with

55. Oywa, interview, July 17, 2017.

56. This description is drawn from "Confidential ACORD-GULU," 27; Oywa, interview, July 17, 2017; Oywa, interview, November 26, 2018; Mbabazi-Mpyangu, "Rebuilding Lives and Relationships," 158–63.

57. Oywa, interview, July 17, 2017. See also Maletta, *Gulu*, 15:13—17:50.

58. Some scholars are more skeptical about the impact of *Mato Oput*. Tim Allen dismisses it as part of a "traditional justice agenda" propagated by Christians and NGO leaders (Allen, "Bitter Roots," 248). Allen also claims that ACORD issued a damning indictment of *Mato Oput* around the year 2000. Whatever ACORD's official views, Rosalba herself was strongly supportive of the revival of these practices in my interviews with her.

59. Oywa, interview, November 26, 2018; Oywa, "International Conference," 4.

60. As she said to a journalist at the time, "This stage after the crisis can be worse than

twenty-one women's groups to lobby the Ugandan government to better integrate gender perspectives into the post-Juba "Peace, Recovery,
and Development Plan" (PRDP).[61] She also contributed to the Makerere
University-based Refugee Law Project's reparations and restorative-justice
initiatives in northern Uganda,[62] and she served internationally as the East
African regional coordinator for the Coalition for Peace for Africa (COPA).
For Oywa, all of this legal and political advocacy work grew from her conviction that issues like land reform and victim compensation should be
framed as questions of justice rather than charity. In her words, "Those are
people's rights; they are not a gift."[63]

Now well into her sixties, Rosalba shows few signs of slowing down.
Every Saturday, she serves as one of three panelists on Gulu radio station
Mega-FM's "Teyat," a program meant to simulate the traditional process
of Acholi elders addressing social challenges "under the tree."[64] She has
been a critical voice in land disputes between local Acholi landowners
and government-banked investors, joining ARPLI leaders in expressing
solidarity with local protesters in Apaa in 2017.[65] As a member of the "Oil
and Gas Commission of the Acholi People," she has spoken out on how
to balance the economic opportunity of oil exploration with the growing
environmental crisis facing Acholiland and Uganda as a whole. In 2018, she
and PVP participated in the inaugural gathering of women's peace activists
at St. Monica's. She also lobbied successfully for a municipal ban on liquor
packets that were causing substantial deaths and addictions among Gulu
youth.[66] Rosalba also continues to contribute to the peacebuilding efforts of

the actual conflict situation if not well handled. We've reached a point where intervention
is crucial, and the outcome can be better or worse, depending on how we intervene as
mothers" ("Uganda Peace," para. 6).

61. See Isis-Women's International Cross-Cultural Exchange, "Women's Task Force."

62. Dolan, interview. Through legal aid, trauma care, and mental health, RLP em-
powers asylum seekers, migrants, refugees, deportees, and IDPs to "enjoy their human
rights and live dignified lives" (See "Refugee Law Project").

63. Oywa, interview, July 17, 2017.

64. Balmoi, interview.

65. Khelil, interview. Concerning a contested boundary between the districts of Ad-
jumani, Moyo, and Acholiland, the Apaa conflict has been one of the most contested and
violent land conflicts in recent years in Uganda. In June 2017, sixteen local protesters
were killed when government officials forcibly demarcated the land boundary. When
Oywa joined ARPRI leaders in their peaceful march to Apaa, they were met with tear gas
and forced to turn back (Balmoi, interview; Khelil, interview).

66. Odong, interview. Rosalba joined seventy-eight other women at St. Rosemary

the Catholic Church. She served on the board of the Archdiocese of Gulu's Justice and Peace Commission between 2006 and 2012 and participates in almost every Dialogue Caravan and Peace Week. A decade after the war ended and most NGOs left the region, Rosalba remains a tireless voice for long-term reconstruction. "After the guns fell silent, this is where the work begins."[67]

Lessons in Catholic Leadership from Rosalba Oywa

Rosalba Oywa offers multiple lessons in Catholic leadership in the public square. First, she reminds Catholics that amidst their charitable relief, political activism, or development work, they should not overlook the importance of social analysis. This entails a recognition of the wider historical and social causes of conflict, such as the destabilizing impacts of the 1970s collapse of the cotton market or the NRM's later destruction of cattle herds in northern Uganda. Notable here is the length of time Rosalba has spent on these issues. In a region where international activists come and go and local activists are at times bought off by the government, Oywa embodies a "rooted activism,"[68] recognizing that northern Uganda's problems require long-term presence and long-term solutions. In the words of John-Bosco Komakech Aludi, current director of Caritas Gulu, Rosalba's number one attribute is that "she is very good and knowledgeable about the situation, and she understands the local context."[69] In sum, if Sr. Rose Muyinza was an exemplar of the charitable Catholic activist, Rosalba Oywa could be a model of the analytical justice activist and grassroots mobilizer. Or in Oywa's words, "What are the root causes of the conflict? And how can we stop the cycle of suffering and handouts?"[70]

Second, like an Old Testament prophet, Rosalba Oywa embodies the importance of truth-telling and especially the willingness to speak truth

Nyrirumbe's inaugural Women's Grassroots Peacebuilding Conference, June 15–16, 2018, sponsored by the University of Oklahoma's Center for Peace and Development.

67. Oywa, interview, November 26, 2018.

68. Dolan, interview.

69. Komakech Aludi, interview. Mega-FM host Steven Balmoi echoed these sentiments. "She [Rosalba] is so rich in information . . . she is knowledgeable in almost every area of peace, governance, health, education, and women's empowerment" (Balmoi, interview).

70. Oywa, interview, July 17, 2017.

to power. Several close associates highlighted Rosalba's "fearlessness" and willingness to "say things as they are" rather than massage her message to make it more politically palatable.[71] In the words of Geoffrey Odong, "her data is a source of power . . . She will not bend low just because you are someone great."[72] For Rosalba, her mission has revolved around a lifelong conviction that the truth will ultimately win. "Lies and propaganda have a short period, but the truth will stand the test of time."[73] And so despite possessing no formal political or military authority, Rosalba sees herself as stronger than the forces arrayed against her. "Knowledge is the greatest source of power. It is better to die for the truth than to remain inactive."[74] Yet her framing of her mission in terms of truth-telling also reflects deeper theological convictions. In particular, Rosalba described herself as one who "bears witness," fully expecting to be judged by God on these grounds. In her words, "If I don't do this, how will I account to God? Supposing I keep quiet even when people trust me so much and give me this information . . . then the consequences could be very bad after my life."[75]

Third, Rosalba's credibility grows from her long-term solidarity with the local people. Her solidarity was forged in personal suffering as she lost relatives, her home, and nearly her own life in the war. Yet to quote Oywa, she, like so many women in northern Uganda, did not remain as victims but rather "turn[ed] their sufferings to become the driving force to risk at times even their own life in search of peace."[76] Like Sherry Meyer and Tonino Pasolini, her solidarity was also forged through decades of on-the-ground presence. Unlike many international activists who flitted in and out of Uganda during and after the war, Rosalba is an example of what Chris Dolan calls the "politics of endurance,"[77] staying with a problem that lacks quick and easy solutions and includes variables well beyond one's control. Her credibility also stemmed from her ability to steer clear of partisan politics. In this sense, Rosalba has resisted some supporters' exhortations to her

71. Dolan, interview; Balmoi, interview.

72. Odong, interview.

73. Oywa, interview, November 26, 2018.

74. Oywa, interview, November 26, 2018.

75. Oywa, interview, November 26, 2018.

76. Oywa, "International Conference," 2.

77. Dolan, interview. Intriguingly, Rosalba herself described the Catholic Church similarly as "the people who stand by us" (Oywa, interview, November 26, 2018).

to run for Parliament, convinced she can better retain both her independence and her circle of influence outside of government.[78]

Again like Pasolini and Meyer, Oywa's leadership focuses on empowering other people and "amplifying" local voices. For Rosalba, a primary mission for both ACORD and PVP was to "give a voice to our people," building trust so that they could speak freely, and then broadcasting these voices for a larger international audience. As a community organizer, Oywa described her role as "a leader of leaders and not a leader of followers," particularly through training youth, women, and traditional religious leaders in mediation and peacebuilding.[79] For Dolan, PVP's name itself is telling. The organization's name is not "Rosalba's Voice for Peace" but "People's Voices for Peace," reflecting her focus on local activism rather than an ego-driven mission to win international humanitarian awards.[80]

Finally, Rosalba Oywa offers a quiet but authentic witness to what one could describe as an "anonymous" Catholic leadership in service to a pluralistic common good. Compared to many of the other Catholic leaders in this book, Oywa did not overtly display her Catholic identity in public. One longtime associate did not even know her religious identity, and even those who described her as a "strong Catholic" agreed that she rarely spoke publicly about her Catholic identity. On one level, this may reflect Rosalba's desire for independence, to be a critical voice not contained within institutions (religious or otherwise). One could also read her as embodying the modern liberal notion that commitment to the interreligious common good requires downplaying religious particularity in the public sphere. But there may be more to it. Rather like Cardinal Nsubuga or Ben Kiwanuka, her Catholic identity is lived out not as a countercultural withdrawal from the world, but rather as a countercultural witness within the world. In turn, in a country with a long history of politico-religious discrimination, it is a religious virtue to "not segregate" on religious grounds, a phrase that was routinely associated with Rosalba.[81] Finally, actions speak louder than words, and empowering others means that one doesn't draw undue attention

78. In the words of Steven Balmoi, "the entire region is her constituency," and her "political party is the Acholi people" (Balmoi, interview).

79. Oywa, interview, July 17, 2017.

80. Dolan, interview.

81. Khelil, interview; Yasinto, interview.

to one's own religiosity. In Oywa's words, "One shouldn't try to shine. If you do your work well, God will find ways to make yourself known."[82]

Ultimately, however, Rosalba Oywa's reticence to present herself as an explicitly "Catholic leader" does not reflect a lack of internal religious conviction. When asked about the spiritual roots of her public activism, she highlighted Christianity's call to reconciliation, especially as embodied in the Lord's Prayer mandate to "forgive us our trespasses as we forgive those who trespass against us."[83] Similarly, Rosalba connected her work as a community organizer to her own understanding of Christian identity. "The feeling that I am giving a voice to the voiceless is important to me as a Christian."[84] On still another occasion, she spoke of the inspiration of the suffering Virgin Mary. "When you look at our Mother Mary, then you know the anguish she went through, and how she had to deal with all the problems of seeing her own Son suffering."[85] A voice of informed analysis on the streets of Gulu, Rosalba Oywa is a witness of Catholic compassion leading to Catholic action.

Reflection Questions

1. How are churches contributing to peacebuilding, reconciliation, or conflict resolution in your own community?

2. What do you see as underlying causes of the biggest social challenges in your community?

3. To what extent should Christians working in the public sphere share their religious or faith convictions?

4. Where do you see yourself "rooted," and what type of social contribution could you make in this place?

82. Oywa, interview, November 26, 2018.
83. Oywa, interview, November 26, 2018.
84. Oywa, interview, November 26, 2018.
85. Oywa, interview, July 17, 2017.

Conclusion

Lessons in Catholic Leadership from Uganda

IN A CONSTRUCTIVE SPIRIT, then, what can we take away from these six case studies in Catholic leadership in modern Uganda? Amidst the evident diversity of personalities, historical eras, apostolates, and regions, are there common threads that we can draw out?

Overall, I would point to five collective "leadership lessons" that emerge from this book. Each reflects key dimensions of Catholic social thought and pastoral emphases in the post-Vatican II context, although I would not argue that these emphases are somehow exclusive to Roman Catholics. And although they emerge out of the unique national context of Uganda, I believe these lessons could also be translated and applied in the North American or other regional contexts.

Lesson One: Embodying Long-Term Solidarity with the Poor and Marginalized

As I stated in the introduction, the opening words of Vatican II's *Gaudium et Spes* capture the spirit of Catholic social leadership described in this book: "The joy and hope, the grief and anguish of the men of our time, especially of those who are poor or afflicted in any way, are the joy and hope, the grief and anguish of the followers of Christ as well. Nothing that is genuinely human fails to find an echo in their hearts." In other words, modern Catholic leaders are called to exercise solidarity and a preferential option *for* and *with* the poor. Fr. John Mary Waliggo, Cardinal Emmanuel Nsubuga, and to a lesser extent Benedicto Kiwanuka embodied the Church's prophetic voice on behalf of the poor; Sr. Rose Muyinza most radically embodied this call to servant-leadership *with* the poor. For their part, Sherry Meyer, Tonino Pasolini and Rosalba Oywa combined these two emphases, both speaking out on behalf of the marginalized and sharing life with them. Even Cardinal Nsubuga spent considerable time in direct contact with the disabled at Nalukolongo. I am struck especially by the long-term nature of these local apostolates of solidarity. Oywa and Muyinza each oversaw local NGOs for over twenty-five years, and Pasolini and Meyer offer eighty combined years of missionary service in one province of Uganda. One is reminded that truly transformative work with the poor does not happen in the short term, and rarely does it happen in a "macro" way. One must work locally, and one must be in it "for the long haul," to echo the language of Chris Rice and Emmanuel Katongole.[1]

Lesson Two: Pursuing a Charismatic Vision within an Institutional Framework

To be honest, I did not anticipate that a book on Ugandan Catholic leadership would end up talking so much about institutions. If anything, I intentionally pivoted away from the institutional focus of so much commentary on the Catholic Church to focus on individual leaders. In turn, most of the leaders in this book could be classified as charismatic visionaries of one kind or the other—people with the power to think outside the box, to use "street smarts" to imagine a new way of approaching an intractable social problem. And yet it would be a mistake to read them as heroic individual warriors. Rather, each responded not by tackling the issue on his or her own, but rather by starting or leading an organization that could address these challenges collectively. Kiwanuka may not have initiated the Democratic Party, but he became the *de facto* founding father of the party, using this as a vehicle to build a new kind of inclusive social politics in Uganda. Nsubuga led an Archdiocese and served as metropolitan bishop for all of Uganda. Waliggo served the Church as a priest yet also recognized the importance of working within national institutions and establishing structures of accountability, whether in the NRM, the Constituent Assembly, or Uganda's Human Rights Commission. Through Radio Pacis, People's Voices for Peace, and Daughters of Charity, Pasolini and Meyer, Oywa, and Muyinza all initiated new organizations that could address emerging challenges of media, peacebuilding, and children's welfare, respectively.

1. Katongole and Rice, *Reconciling All Things*, 143–46.

Perhaps most importantly, the long-term success and failure of these leaders was intrinsically intertwined with the success and failure of their organizations. For all of her charisma, vision, and personal holiness, Muyinza struggled with management, delegation, and administration; not surprisingly the Daughters of Charity have struggled since her death. In contrast, Pasolini and Meyer established employment practices and organizational structures to reinforce Radio Pacis's team-based culture of mutual accountability, enabling the organization to thrive even as its founders pull back. This reminds us that for all of the challenges and negative associations with the "institutional church," especially in my own American context, institutions are necessary to sustain theological vision.[2] Likewise, creative charisma is necessary to ensure that Christian organizations or communities don't "quench the Spirit" (1 Thess 5:19), reading new "signs of the times" in the light of the gospel (*Gaudium et Spes* 4).

Lesson Three: Empowering Others through Servant-Leadership

For all of Lesson Two's emphasis on individual creativity and organizational management, successful Ugandan Catholic leaders have recognized the importance of empowering others and, to quote a friend of Fr. Waliggo, "leading from behind." In other words, the most effective pastoral leaders are not necessarily garnering headlines, seeking public attention, or leading out in front. One thinks here of colleagues' descriptions of Rosalba Oywa as "not seeking after attention," or Sr. Rose Muyinza as "not presenting herself as a big person." Whatever their clerical privileges and public contributions, friends of Fr. Waliggo and Cardinal Nsubuga smiled most broadly when recalling how each could mingle joyfully with ordinary people. Likewise, many of the leaders profiled in these pages were remembered for how they lifted others up. Oywa's PVP brought ordinary Acholi women's voices into the peacebuilding conversation; Sr. Muyinza helped individuals turn their lives around through education and vocational training; Fr. Waliggo was renowned for his mentoring work, whether of fellow priests or colleagues at Uganda's Human Rights office. For Waliggo, mentoring was in fact the very

---

2. In the words of the social scientist Eric Morier-Genoud, writing on the Mozambique context, "one could argue that institutionalizing internal diversity is what makes the Catholic Church unique and also makes all sorts of futures possible for the church" (*Catholicism and the Making of Politics*, 173).

measure of a good leader: "The success of a good leader is detected through the person who succeeds him."[3]

In their lay ministry training and at Radio Pacis, Meyer and Pasolini perhaps best embody what Catholic leadership writer Anthony d'Souza, SJ calls the "four Es" of genuine empowerment: ennobling, enabling, empowering and encouraging. In D'Souza's words, "to ennoble is to transmit or impart the significance and purpose of people and their work . . . To enable is to provide the tools, knowledge, equipment, and the capability necessary to do the work."[4] For D'Souza, one can empower people—namely "grant them the license for action while at the same time invoking the responsibility for their actions"[5]—after you've built up their dignity and trained them in the necessary skills. This is then sustained by a hands-on, encouraging culture that facilitates honest feedback within an environment of mutual care and concern. Radio Pacis's Friday meeting tradition serves a critical role here, giving all staff opportunities to voice commendations, critiques, and challenges that warrant further attention or a fresh approach.

In more theological terms, however, these leaders embody the age-old Christian call to servant-leadership. They understood that genuine Christian leadership does not entail lording it over the community but giving oneself in service to the community. In this sense, they live into Jesus's own countercultural teachings in the Gospel of Luke: "The kings of the Gentiles lord it over them and those in authority over them are addressed as 'Benefactors'; but among you it shall not be so. Rather, let the greatest among you be as the youngest, and the leader as the servant" (Luke 22:25–26).

Lesson Four: Seeking Truth and Justice with the Self-Sacrificial Spirit of the Martyrs

Perhaps more than any other Christian country in the modern world, Uganda has been profoundly shaped by the culture and spirit of religious martyrdom. In many major Catholic parishes in Uganda, the crucifix above the altar is surrounded by a mosaic of the Uganda Martyrs. Schools and priests take their names from martyrs such as St. Kizito, St. Charles Lwanga, or St. Joseph Balikuddembe. The June 3 feast of the Uganda Martyrs is the annual highlight of the Catholic calendar and a national holiday for all

3. Nanseera, interview.

4. D'Souza, *Leaders for Today*, 159.

5. D'Souza, *Leaders for Today*, 160.

Ugandans. Other martyr traditions—such as those surrounding the Acholi catechists Daudi Okelo and Jildo Irwa—have also developed strong devotional followings in recent years.[6]

Not surprisingly, a major theme in this book has been the martyr's spirit of sacrificial leadership in commitment to perceived gospel truth. Benedicto Kiwanuka perhaps best embodies this ethos. "Truth and Justice" were the backbone principles of his Democratic Party, and he refused opportunities to flee into exile or avoid political martyrdom due to his convictions. As he said in one of his last communications with friends, "We cannot allow our country to continue in this way because we are too threatened. If we have to die, let's die as martyrs rather than as cowards."[7] The martyr's spirit is also reflected in the witness of Sr. Rose Muyinza, whose austere lifestyle and tireless work ethic echoed the "white martyrdom" often associated with desert monasticism in the early church. But one also sees a martyr's emphasis on truth in the courageous witness of Rosalba Oywa, convinced that "lies and propaganda have a short period, but truth will stand the test of time."[8] For all of his collaboration with government, Fr. Waliggo was known for his willingness to speak out on injustices inside the halls of NRM power; several colleagues attributed Uganda's recent growth in corruption and authoritarianism in part to the absence of Waliggo's critical internal voice. In his public letters, Cardinal Nsubuga voiced this commitment to speaking truth to power, especially during the Obote II years when he may have been the most respected and influential anti-government voice in the country. Likewise, Radio Pacis was founded in part to counter media misinformation, recognizing that if "what is said on the radio is taken as gospel truth,"[9] Catholic radio stations better make sure they are speaking truth.

6. Okelo and Irwa were killed in 1918, and their cause has boomed in popularity over the past thirty years in the midst of the LRA war and its aftermath (Alava, "There is Confusion," 62–65). On the original history of the Paimol martyrs, see Cisternino, *Passion for Africa*, 475–87.

7. "Bendicto Kagimu Mugumba Kiwanuka," 26; Bade, *Benedicto Kiwanuka*, 158.

8. Oywa, interview, November 26, 2018.

9. Idraku, interview.

Lesson Five: The More "Catholic," the More "catholic": The Ambivalence of the Catholic Common Good Mission

Finally, the leaders profiled in these pages embody modern Catholic social teaching's emphasis on service to the common good. Since Vatican II, Church politics has moved away from the anti-modern and "defending Catholic interests" postures so characteristic of the nineteenth and early twentieth centuries, and toward a constructive and collaborative engagement with modernity in service to the common people. Latin American liberation theologians advocated for the poor, not just Catholics; the Polish Solidarity movement opposed Communism on behalf of workers and the Polish people; the US Catholic Bishops Conference calls on Catholics to vote and actively participate in American democracy in accordance with their conscience and in service to the common good. With this mainstreaming of social Catholicism, there has been a concomitant sacrifice of particularity. In my own American context, the "Catholic subculture," a distinctive social ethos that shaped generations of ninteenth- and early twentieth-century American immigrants, has collapsed, and there are few social, educational, or economic differences between American Catholics and other Americans. Ideological and ethnic differences are now far more determinative.

Likewise in Uganda, most of the leaders profiled in these pages worked for the national common good and downplayed Catholic particularity. Whatever his personal devotion or the dominant presence of Catholics in his party, Kiwanuka repeatedly denied that DP was a "Catholic party," preferring to describe it in more general terms such as "a band of well-intentioned men and women out to do good."[10] Rosalba Oywa's activism largely unfolded outside the Church; some colleagues did not even know she was a Catholic. Even priests like Fr. Waliggo were remembered for being "liberal," "down-to-earth," and comfortable in secular work contexts; "you wouldn't think that he was a priest," as one colleague recalled. In turn, all of these leaders embraced ministries that touched not just Catholics. Sr. Muyinza's Daughters of Charity practiced Catholic devotions but also accepted young people from all religious denominations, even allowing Muslims to attend Friday prayers at the mosque. Radio Pacis begins its staff meetings with reflection on the upcoming Sunday gospel yet also hires Muslims, Protestants, and those of no faith. In Archbishop Nsubuga's famous words at his

---

10. "D. P. Leader's Appeal," 2.

1966 installation, "I am not just for the Catholics—I am for you all." There is much to commend in this "common good Catholicism," especially in Uganda where religious divisions exercised such doleful effects for so many decades. Significantly, the motto of "For God and my Country" does not read "For God, my Church, and my Country."

And yet there may be a cost here. In Uganda, there is little sense of the Church offering a distinctive community or sociopolitical mission outside of aiding the nation-state; modern nationalist mythos goes largely unchallenged in Ugandan religious discourse. Rare is the recognition of the inherent ambiguity—perhaps even contradiction—in simultaneously trying to serve both "God" and "Country." In this regard, the Ugandan Church fulfills what Emmanuel Katongole calls the "pious," "political," and "pastoral" postures of church-state relations, emphasizing service and loyalty as a development partner for the state. Yet in its "obsession with relevance," the Church may be underwriting what Katongole calls a "Christianity without consequences"—namely failing in its responsibility to offer an alternative witness to God's inaugurated kingdom in the world, a "church as a resurrected and strange communion of witnesses drawn from all tribes, nations and languages."[11] In turn, as has been seen in European and American culture since the 1960s, the loss of the Catholic subculture can undergird growing secularism, and with this the resurgence of even more particularistic religious identities. Uganda is far from this Western reality, but rapid modernization, the current boom in transnational social media and entertainment, and the recent rise of both Born-Again Pentecostalism and radical currents of Islam on the continent could shift this dynamic in the twenty-first century.

I would argue in closing, however, that Catholics in Uganda or the USA should neither deny nor fear the inherent ambivalence of public leadership. The Catholic tradition is a "both-and" rather than an "either-or" tradition, embracing Scripture *and* tradition, faith *and* works, grace *and* nature, Christ's humanity *and* divinity. The proper theological approach here is not to eliminate one truth in favor of the other, but to hold both truths simultaneously, with all of the delicate tension this entails. In this regard, one important "both-and" that emerges in these chapters is "Catholic" and "catholic." All of these leaders' lives have been deeply shaped by the particularity of the institutional *Catholic* Church, especially through primary and secondary schooling, sacramental practice, spiritual devotions,

11. Katongole, *Mirror to the Church*, 88, 123, 127.

church-based social institutions, and the Church's social teaching. Yet all also reflect the original meaning of the word "*catholic*" in the Greek word *katholikos*, or "universal," living their lives in service and solidarity with the broader community beyond the church.

To play on words, "the more Catholic, the more catholic"—the deepening of one's Catholic spirituality should ultimately lead one outward, calling the leader to be a self-gift on behalf of the community. Such a journey is by no means inevitable, nor is it without ambivalence or ambiguity. But we can be grateful for leaders like Kiwanuka, Nsubuga, Muyinza, Waliggo, Meyer, Pasolini, and Oywa, each of whom has radiated self-sacrificial, *agapic* love on behalf of their people.

Bibliography

Abide. "Our Mission." https://www.abideomaha.org/our-mission.

Acan, Grace. *Not Yet Sunset: A Story of Survival and Perseverance in LRA Captivity.* Kampala, Uganda: Fountain, 2017.

Adrapi, Gabriel (Field reporter with Radio Pacis). Interview by author, Radio Pacis, Arua, Uganda, October 10, 2018.

Agostoni, Tarcisio. Correspondence to Benedicto Kiwanuka, July 8, 1959. Chief Minister's Office, 1949–72/Chief Minister's Personal Correspondence folder, BKMKP.

———. Correspondence to Benedicto Kiwanuka, July 4, 1971. Mr. Kiwanuka Personal folder, BKMKP.

———. *Every Citizen's Handbook.* Nairobi: Paulines Publications Africa, 1962, 1997.

Aizenman, Nurith, and Gharib, Malaka. "American with No Medical Training Ran Center for Malnourished Ugandan Kids. 105 Died." *National Public Radio,* August 9, 2019. https://www.npr.org/sections/goatsandsoda/2019/08/09/749005287/american-with-no-medical-training-ran-center-for-malnourished-ugandan-kids-105-d.

Akwacha, Man'gwe. "You Cannot have Two Masters in One Home." *Uganda Argus,* December 27, 1961.

Alava, Henni. "There is Confusion: The Politics of Silence, Fear and Hope in Catholic and Protestant Northern Uganda." PhD diss., University of Helsinki, 2017.

"All Asians Must Go." *Uganda Argus,* August 21, 1972. Annotated Newspapers folder, BKMKP.

Allen, Tim. "Bitter Roots: The Invention of Acholi Traditional Justice." In *The Lord's Resistance Army: Myth and Reality,* edited by Tim Allen and Koen Vlassenroot, 242–61. London: Zed, 2010.

Allen, Tim, and Koen Vlassenroot, eds. *The Lord's Resistance Army: Myth and Reality.* London: Zed, 2010.

Amooti, Jones Mugume (former staff with Daughters of Charity's Kiwanga home). Interview by author, Kampala, Uganda, February 5, 2019.

Amviko, Sarah (human resources manager at Radio Pacis). Interview with author, Arua, Uganda, July 3, 2017.

———. Interview with author, Radio Pacis, Arua, Uganda, October 10, 2018.

Anderson, Gerald. "A Moratorium on Missionaries?" *The Christian Century,* January 16, 1974. https://www.religion-online.org/article/a-moratorium-on-missionaries/.

Apamaku, Gaetano (station manager at Radio Pacis). Email communication with author, June 24, 2019.

———. Interview by author, Arua, Uganda, July 3, 2017.

"Appendix B to Gen Order 1100 of 1944." August 29, 1945. Villa Marie O. B. Association folder, BKMKP.

Archdiocese of Kampala. "2006 Report on the Daughters of Charity." Unpublished paper, September 27, 2006.

Aroga, Paul (field reporter for Radio Pacis). Interview by author, Burua, Arua district, Uganda, October 7, 2018.

Arrupe, Pedro. "Men for Others: Education for Social Justice and Social Action Today, 1973, Valencia, Spain." http://onlineministries.creighton.edu/CollaborativeMinistry/men-for-others.html.

Atule, Moses (chief news editor, Radio Pacis). Interview by author, Radio Pacis, Arua, Uganda, October 8, 2018.

Avoku, Tonny (public relations and sales manager, Radio Pacis). Interview by author, Radio Pacis, Arua, Uganda, October 10, 2018.

Ayikobua, Noel (programs manager, Radio Pacis). Interview by author, Radio Pacis, Arua, Uganda, July 3, 2017.

———. Interview by author, Radio Pacis, Arua, Uganda, October 10, 2018.

Babirye, Justine (former beneficiary of Sr. Rose Muyinza's Daughters of Charity). Interview by author, Kampala, Uganda, July 5, 2017.

Bade, Albert. *Benedicto Kiwanuka: The Man and His Politics*. Kampala: Fountain, 1996.

Balmoi, Steven (radio host, Mega-FM Gulu). Interview by author, Gulu, Uganda, November 25, 2018.

Baltz, David (Comboni priest and former missionary in West Nile district). Interview by author, Omaha, Nebraska, June 17, 2018.

Baltz, David, and Tonino Pasolini. Interview by author, Radio Pacis, Arua, Uganda, July 1, 2015.

Baptist, Rwot Latim (Pawel clan chief, Acholiland). Interview by author, Gulu, Uganda, November 27, 2018.

Basemera, Theresa (Good Samaritan Sister, former administrator of Nalukolongo Home, and director of Kiwanga Integrated Skills Training Center). Interview by author, Nalukolongo, Kampala, Uganda, June 30, 2015.

———. Interview by author, Kiwanga Integrated Skills Training Center, Jinja Road, Uganda, July 8, 2017.

Baur, John. *2000 Years of Christianity in Africa: An African Church History*. Rev. ed. Nairobi: Paulines Publications Africa, 2009.

Bediako, Kwame. *Christianity in Africa: The Renewal of a Non-Western Religion*. Edinburgh: Edinburgh University Press, 1995.

Behrend, Heike. *Alice Lakwena and the Holy Spirits: War in Northern Uganda, 1986–97*. Athens: Ohio University Press, 2000.

"Bendicto Kagimu Mugumba Kiwanuka: A Martyr of Truth and Justice. A Proposal Submitted to the Ordinary of Kampala Archdiocese to Open a Formal Process for the Beatification of the Late Bendicto Kagimu Mugumba Kiwanuka." Kampala: N.P., 2015.

Benedict XVI. *Africae Munus: On the Church in Africa in Service to Reconciliation, Justice and Peace*. Post-synodal apostolic exhortation, 2011. http://www.vatican.va/content/benedict-xvi/en/apost_exhortations/documents/hf_ben-xvi_exh_20111119_africae-munus.html.

Biko, Steven. *Black Consciousness in South Africa*. Edited by Millard Arnold. New York: Vintage, 1979.

Birungi, Natal Gloria (former beneficiary of Daughters of Charity). Interview by author, Kampala, Uganda, February 10, 2019.

Boesak, Alan. *Farewell to Innocence: A Socio-ethical Study on Black Theology and Power.* Maryknoll, NY: Orbis, 1977.

Bosa, Elizabeth (former personal secretary to John Mary Waliggo). Interview by author, Kampala, Uganda, April 17, 2019.

Boyle, Gregory. *Tattoos on the Heart: The Power of Boundless Compassion.* New York: Simon and Schuster, 2010.

Buchanan, Tom, and Martin Conway, eds. *Political Catholicism in Europe, 1918–1965.* Oxford: Clarendon, 1996.

Budde, Michael L., and Karen Scott, eds. *Witness of the Body: The Past, Present, and Future of Christian Martyrdom.* Grand Rapids: Eerdmans, 2011.

Bugembe, Patrick (cousin of John Mary Waliggo). Interview by author, Kampala, Uganda, April 24, 2019.

Bujo, Bénézet. *African Christian Morality at the Age of Inculturation.* Nairobi: Paulines Publications Africa, 1990.

Buthelezi, Manas. "An African Theology or a Black Theology?" In *The Challenge of Black Theology in South Africa*, edited by Basil Moore, 29–35. Atlanta: John Knox, 1973.

Byamukama, Nathan (former colleague of John Mary Waliggo at Uganda Human Rights Commission). Interview by author, Munyonyo, Kampala, Uganda, March 15, 2019.

Carney, J. J. "'The Bishop is Governor Here': Bishop Nicholas Djomo and Catholic Leadership in the Democratic Republic of the Congo." In *Leadership in Postcolonial Africa: Trends Transformed by Independence*, edited by Baba G. Jallow, 97–122. New York: Palgrave Macmillan, 2015.

———. "The People Bonded Together by Love: Eucharistic Ecclesiology and Small Christian Communities in Africa." *Modern Theology* 30 (2014) 300–18.

———. *Rwanda Before the Genocide: Catholic Politics and Ethnic Discourse in the Late Colonial Era.* New York: Oxford University Press, 2014.

CELAM (Latin American Episcopal Conference). "Document on the Poverty of the Church." In *Liberation Theology: A Documentary History*, edited by Alfred Hennelly, 114–19. Maryknoll, NY: Orbis, 1992.

Cisternino, Mario. *Passion for Africa: Missionary and Imperial Papers on the Evangelisation of Uganda and Sudan, 1848–1923.* Kampala: Fountain, 2004.

"Confidential ACORD-GULU: A Survey of Causes, Effects and Impacts of Armed Conflict in Gulu District." Unpublished paper, April 1997.

Dada, Romanus. "Comboni Day Lecture," Comboni Sisters' Residence, Arua, Uganda, October 10, 2018.

———. Interview by author, Christus Centre, Arua, Uganda, July 3, 2017.

D'Antonio, William. "US Catholics Weigh in on 2016 Election in New Survey." *National Catholic Reporter*, November 1, 2017. https://www.ncronline.org/news/politics/us-catholics-weigh-2016-election-new-survey.

Ddembe, Joseph (staff member at Sabina School and former associate of Sr. Rose Muyinza). Interview by author, Rakai, Uganda, February 10, 2019.

"Democratic Party 13-Point Programme of Priorities from Our Manifesto." December 1, 1960. Not Marked 5 folder, BKMKP.

"Democratic Party Manifesto: Forward to Freedom." April 11, 1960. UG.DP.39 folder, ICS-PP.

De Temmeran, Els. *Aboke Girls: Children Abducted in Northern Uganda.* Kampala: Fountain, 2009.

"Detention Notice to Benedicto Kiwanuka." December 22, 1970. Confidential 2 folder, BKMKP.

Dolan, Chris (director, Refugee Law Project). Interview by author, Kampala, Uganda, October 30, 2018.

Dotzler, Ron. Interview by author, Omaha, Nebraska, July 5, 2016.

———. *Out of the Seats and into the Streets*. Self-published: CreateSpace, 2015.

"D.P. Leader's Appeal." *Uganda Argus*, September 30, 1958.

D'Souza, Anthony. *Leaders for Today, Hope for Tomorrow: Empowering and Empowered Leadership*. Nairobi: Paulines Publications Africa, 2004.

Earle, Jonathon L. *Colonial Buganda and the End of Empire*. Cambridge: Cambridge University Press, 2017.

Eboussi-Boulaga, Fabien. *Christianity without Fetishes*. Maryknoll, NY: Orbis, 1984.

Éla, Jean-Marc. *African Cry*. Maryknoll, NY: Orbis, 1986.

"Expulsion of Priests Raises Problems." *The Daily Nation*, Kampala, Uganda, January 20, 1967.

Faupel, J. F. *African Holocaust: The Story of the Uganda Martyrs*. New York: P. J. Kennedy, 1962.

Fernandez de Aller, Fidel Gonzales. "La Idea Misionera de Daniel Comboni, Primer Vicario Apostolico del Africa Central, en el Contexto Socio-Eclesial del Siglo XIX." ThD diss., Universidad Pontificia de Salamanca, 1979.

Ford, Margaret. *Janani: The Making of a Martyr*. London: Lakeland, 1978.

Foster, Elizabeth. *African Catholic: Decolonization and the Transformation of the Church*. Cambridge: Harvard University Press, 2019.

"The Four Religious Leaders' Concern Over the Current Affairs in Uganda." July 9, 1979, Dossier 995, Folio 79, RDA.

Francis. *Evangelii Gaudium*: The Joy of the Gospel. Apostolic exhortation, November 24, 2013. http://www.vatican.va/content/francesco/en/apost_exhortations/documents/papa-francesco_esortazione-ap_20131124_evangelii-gaudium.html.

Freire, Paolo. *The Pedagogy of the Oppressed*. New York: Bloomsbury Academic, 2000.

"From Bonn to (British) Foreign Office." November 2, 1960. 1960 Kiwanuka DP folder, PRO CO 822-2119.

Gavamukulya, Albert (professor of spirituality at St. Mary's Ggaba National Seminary). Interview by author, Ggaba, Kampala, Uganda, June 2, 2015.

Gbowee, Leymah. *Mighty Be Our Powers: How Sisterhood, Prayer, and Sex Changed a Nation at War*. New York: Beast, 2011.

Gifford, Paul. *African Christianity: Its Public Role*. Bloomington: Indiana University Press, 1998.

———. *Christianity, Development and Modernity in Africa*. New York: Oxford University Press, 2016.

Gilli, Aldo. *Daniel Comboni: The Man and His Message*. Bologna: Editrice Missionaria Italiana, 1980.

Gutièrrez, Gustavo. *A Theology of Liberation*. Maryknoll, NY: Orbis, 1971.

Hansen, Holger B. "The Colonial State's Policy Toward Foreign Missions in Uganda." In *Christian Missionaries and the State in the Third World*, edited by Holger B. Hansen and Michael Twaddle, 157–75. Oxford: James Currey, 2002.

———. *Mission, Church, and State in a Colonial Setting: Uganda 1890–1925*. London: Heinemann, 1984.

Hastings, Adrian. *The Church in Africa 1450–1950*. Oxford: Oxford University Press, 1994.

———— *A History of African Christianity 1950–1975*. Cambridge: Cambridge University Press, 1979.

Healey, Joseph G. "Basic Christian Communities: Church-centered or World-centered?" *Missionalia* 1 (1986) 14–32.

Hoekema, David A. "Risking Peace: How Religious Leaders Ended Uganda's Civil War." *Commonweal Magazine*, January 3, 2019. https://www.commonwealmagazine.org/risking-peace.

————. *We are the Voice of the Grass: Interfaith Peace Activism in Northern Uganda*. New York: Oxford University Press, 2019.

Horn, Gerd-Rainer. *Western European Liberation Theology: The First Wave (1924–1959)*. Oxford: Oxford University Press, 2008.

Idraku, Charles (assistant director at Radio Pacis). Interview by author, Radio Pacis, Arua, Uganda, May 13, 2019.

Ingham, Kenneth. *Obote: A Political Biography*. London: Routledge, 1994.

Inspector General of Police. Correspondence to Benedicto Kiwanuka, December 20, 1962. In Confidential 2/G.A. Anderson folder, BKMKP.

Isis-Women's International Cross-Cultural Exchange. "Women's Task Force for a Gender-Responsive PRDP: Policy Brief, Recommendations for a gender responsive Peace, Recovery, and Development Plan for North and North Eastern Uganda (PRDP)." Working paper, November 2009.

"J. Kiwanuka Statement at Namirembe Constitutional Conference, 3 August 1954." In *The Mind of Buganda: Documents of the Modern History of an African Kingdom*, edited by Donald A. Low, 176. London: Heinemann, 1971.

John XXIII. "Pope John's Opening Speech to the Council, 11 October 1962." http://vatican2voice.org/91docs/opening_speech.htm.

John Paul II. *Sollicitudo Rei Socialis* (On Social Concern). Encyclical letter, December 30, 1987. http://www.vatican.va/content/john-paul-ii/en/encyclicals/documents/hf_jp-ii_enc_30121987_sollicitudo-rei-socialis.html.

Johnson, Douglas H. *South Sudan: A New History for a New Nation*. Athens: Ohio University Press, 2016.

"Kabaka Orders: Arrest Prelate: Crowds gather to protest at Rubaga." *Uganda Argus*, November 25, 1961.

Kabuye, John Bosco (former beneficiary with Sr. Rose Muyinza's Daughters of Charity). Interview by author, Luweero, Uganda, April 27, 2019.

Kaggwa, Med S. K. (former chair of Ugandan Human Rights Commission and associate of J. M. Waliggo in constitutional revision process). Interview with author, Kampala, Uganda, March 1, 2019.

Kahooza, Grace (former collaborator with Sr. Rose Muyinza and Daughters of Charity). Interview by author, Kampala, Uganda, February 27, 2019.

Kaiser, Wolfram. *Christian Democracy and the Origins of the European Union*. Cambridge: Cambridge University Press, 2007.

Kalyabbe, Joseph (retired priest, Diocese of Kasana-Luweero). Interview by author, Luweero, Uganda, May 28, 2015.

Kamya, John (commander of Senior Police Command and Staff College for the Uganda Police Force). Interview by author, Bujagaala, Uganda, March 12, 2019.

Kanyandago, Peter. "John Mary Waliggo: The Theology of John Mary Waliggo." In *African Theology: The Contribution of the Pioneers*, edited by Bénézet Bujo and Juvénal Ilunga Muya, 215–30. Nairobi: Paulines Publications Africa, 2006.

Kanyerezi, Matthias (retired vicar general, Diocese of Kasana-Luweero). Interview with author, Luweero, Uganda, June 20, 2015.

Karugire, Samwiri R. *A Political History of Uganda*. Nairobi: Heinemann, 1980.

Kasibante, Charles (vicar general of Archdiocese of Kampala and former pastor of Christ the King Parish, Kampala). Interview by author, Nsambya, Kampala, Uganda, April 17, 2019.

Kasozi, A. B. K. *The Social Origins of Violence in Uganda 1964–85*. Montreal: McGill-Queen's University Press, 1994.

Kassimir, Ronald. "Complex Martyrs: Symbols of Catholic Church Formation and Political Differentiation in Uganda." *African Affairs* 90.360 (1991) 357–82.

Kasule, Joseph (priest and former classmate of J. M. Waliggo at Bukalasa Minor Seminary). Interview by author, Masaka, Uganda, December 12, 2018.

Katongole, Emmanuel. *Born from Lament: The Theology and Politics of Hope in Africa*. Grand Rapids: Eerdmans, 2017.

———. *The Journey of Reconciliation: Groaning for a New Creation in Africa*. Maryknoll, NY: Orbis, 2017.

———. *Mirror to the Church: Resurrecting Faith after Genocide in Rwanda*. Grand Rapids: Zondervan, 2009.

———. *The Sacrifice of Africa: A Political Theology for Africa*. Grand Rapids: Eerdmans, 2011.

Katongole, Emmanuel, and Chris P. Rice. *Reconciling All Things: A Christian Vision for Justice, Peace, and Healing*. Downers Grove, IL: InterVarsity, 2008.

Kennedy, John F. "Address to the Greater Houston Ministerial Association." September 12, 1960, John F. Kennedy Presidential Library and Museum, transcript and mp4, 11:19. https://www.jfklibrary.org/learn/about-jfk/historic-speeches/address-to-the-greater-houston-ministerial-association.

Khelil, Sheikh Musa (regional khadi of the Uganda Muslim Supreme Council in northern Uganda). Interview by author, Gulu, Uganda, November 28, 2018.

Kibirango, Leo (former president of Bank of Uganda and chair of board of trustees, Daughters of Charity). Interview by author, Kampala, Uganda, July 11, 2017.

Kimbowa, Charles M. *Emmanuel Cardinal Kiwanuka Nsubuga Still Lives with Us*. Kisubi, Uganda: Marianum, 2005.

———. (former personal secretary to Cardinal Emmanuel Nsubuga). Interview by author, Nsambya, Kampala, June 25, 2015.

Kittel, Gerhard, and Gerhard Friedrich, eds. *Theological Dictionary of the New Testament*. Abridged in One Volume. Translated by Geoffrey W. Bromiley. Grand Rapids: Eerdmans, 1985.

Kituuma, Herman (rector of St. Thomas Katigondo Major Seminary). Interview by author, Katigondo, Masaka, Uganda, December 12, 2018.

Kivengere, Festo. *I Love Idi Amin: A Story of Triumph under Fire in the Midst of Suffering and Persecution in Uganda*. Old Tappan, NJ: New Life Ventures, 1977.

Kiwanuka, Benedicto K. M. "Address at International Conference Center." July 7, 1971. Private Correspondence folder, BKMKP.

———. Correspondence to Aloysius Lugira. February 5, 1972, Mr. Kiwanuka personal folder, BKMKP.

———. Correspondence to Editor of *Catholic Herald* newspaper (U.K.). February 27, 1954. Villa Marie O.B. Association folder, BKMKP.

———. Correspondence to E. M. K. Mulira. August 25, 1969. Confidential 2 folder, BKMKP.

———. Correspondence to Geoffrey Fisher. October 1961. Federal Status folder, BKMKP.

———. Correspondence to Idi Amin Dada. February 4, 1971. Elections folder, BKMKP.

———. Correspondence to Idi Amin Dada. August 31, 1972. Govt House Copies of Minutes folder, BKMKP.

———. Correspondence to Milton Obote. May 20, 1964. Confidential 2 folder, BKMKP.

———. Correspondence to Milton Obote. March 3, 1966. Confidential 2 folder, BKMKP.

———. Correspondence to Rector of St. Thomas National Seminary Katigondo. August 17, 1953. Govt House Copies of Minutes folder, BKMKP.

———. "DP Presidential Address 1959." August 7, 1959. Uganda Versus folder, BKMKP.

———. "DP Response to State of Emergency." November 14, 1966. Uganda Versus folder, BKMKP.

———. "Handwritten note on Uganda's political situation." n.d., Not Marked 6 folder, BKMKP.

———. "Presidential Address." August 20, 1960, Confidential 1 folder, BKMKP.

———. "Uganda Elections–1962." Dossier 904, Folder 4, RDA.

———. "Views on Forms of Government and Head of State." April 11, 1960, Not Marked 5 folder, BKMKP.

———. "What Happened in London: Federal Status for Kingdoms." 1962. Uganda Versus folder, BKMKP.

Kiwanuka, Henry Nsubuga (nephew of Emmanuel Cardinal Nsubuga). Phone interview by author, August 20, 2015.

Kiwanuka, Joseph. "Church and State: Guiding Principles." Pastoral Letter, Archdiocese of Rubaga, November 23, 1961.

Kiwanuka, Maurice Kagimu (son of Benedicto Kiwanuka). "Address." Benedicto Kiwanuka Inaugural Memorial Lecture. Public speech attended by author, High Court, Kampala, Uganda, September 21, 2018.

———. Interview by author, Rubaga, Kampala, Uganda, July 6, 2017.

Kiwanuka, Regina (daughter of Benedicto Kiwanuka). Interview by author, Kampala, Uganda, May 8, 2019.

Kollman, Paul V. *The Evangelization of Slaves and Catholic Origins in Eastern Africa.* Maryknoll, NY: Orbis, 2005.

Kollman, Paul V., and Cynthia Toms Smedley. *Understanding World Christianity: Eastern Africa.* Minneapolis: Fortress, 2018.

Komakech Aludi, John Bosco (director of Caritas, Archdiocese of Gulu). Phone interview by author, Kampala, Uganda, July 21, 2017.

Kyemba, Henry. *A State of Blood: The Inside Story of Idi Amin.* New York: Ace, 1977.

Leeming, Donald, et al. *History of East Africa.* Harlow, UK: Longman, 2010.

Longman Dictionary of Contemporary English. "The Streets." https://www.ldoceonline. com/dictionary/the-streets.

Low, Donald A. *Buganda in Modern History.* Berkeley: University of California Press, 1971.

———. "Uganda Unhinged." *International Affairs* 49, no. 2 (1973) 219–28.

Lubega, Teo (former board member of Daughters of Charity and collaborator with Sr. Rose Muyinza). Interview by author, Kampala, Uganda, February 5, 2019.

Lugira, Aloysius M. "The Catholic Church and Development in Uganda: A Tribute to the late Hon. Benedicto Kagimu Mugumba Kiwanuka." December 4, 1999. https://www2.bc.edu/aloysius-lugira/churchdev.htm.

Luwum, Janani, and Emmanuel Nsubuga. "UJCC Memorandum on Behalf of the Executive Committee to His Excellency the President of Uganda, May 1975." Reel 72, Office of the Archbishop folder, ACU.

Lwanga Lunyiigo, Samwiiri. Interview by author, Kisubi, Uganda, September 29, 2018.

Magesa, Laurenti. *Anatomy of Inculturation: Transforming the Church in Africa*. Maryknoll, NY: Orbis, 2004.

———. "The Theological Legacy of John Mary Waliggo." In *Catholic Church Leadership in Peacebuilding in Africa*, edited by Elias O. Opongo and David Kaulema, 62–71. Nairobi: Paulines Publications Africa, 2014.

———. *What is Not Sacred? African Spirituality*. Maryknoll, NY: Orbis, 2013.

Magunda, Darius (professor of church history at St. Mbaagaa National Seminary). Interview with author, Ggaba, Kampala, Uganda, June 2, 2015.

Maletta, Robert, dir. *Gulu: The Struggle for Peace*. 1999; Little Rock, AR: Trojan Horse Productions. Responding to Conflict Series. https://vimeo.com/9697961.

Marsh, Charles. *The Beloved Community: How Faith Shapes Social Justice from the Civil Rights Movement to Today*. New York: Basic, 2005.

Martin, Phyllis. *Catholic Women of Congo-Brazzaville: Mothers and Sisters in Troubled Times*. Bloomington: Indiana University Press, 2009.

Mary Cleophas (Little Sister of St. Francis). Interview by author, Nkokonjeru, Uganda, July 13, 2017.

Massaro, Thomas. *Living Justice: Catholic Social Teaching in Action*. 3rd ed. Lanham, MD: Rowman and Littlefield, 2016.

Matovu, Fred (former property administrator with Daughters of Charity). Interview by author, Nsambya, Kampala, Uganda, April 29, 2019.

Matzko McCarthy, David, ed. *The Heart of Catholic Social Teaching: Its Origins and Contemporary Significance*. Grand Rapids: Brazos, 2009.

Mayanja, Denis (retired priest and associate of John Mary Waliggo). Interview with author, Masaka, Uganda, December 12, 2018.

Mayanja, Fred (former Daughters of Charity beneficiary and headmaster of Kiwanga school). Interview by author, Bweyogerere, Uganda, May 1, 2019.

Mbabazi-Mpyangu, Christine. "Rebuilding Lives and Relationships through Forgiveness and Reconciliation in Northern Uganda." In *The Ugandan Churches and the Political Centre: Cooperation, Co-option, and Confrontation*, edited by Paddy Musana Angus Crichton and Caroline Howell, 151–70. Cambridge: Ngoma Ecumenical Publishing Consortium and Cambridge Centre for Christianity Worldwide, 2017.

McElwee, Joshua J. "Pope Francis: 'I Would Love a Church that is Poor.'" *National Catholic Reporter*, March 16, 2013. https://www.ncronline.org/blogs/francis-chronicles/pope-francis-i-would-love-church-poor.

McNeill, Donald P., et al. *Compassion: A Reflection on the Christian Life*. Garden City, NY: Doubleday, 1982.

Meyer, Sherry. Interview by author, Radio Pacis, Arua, Uganda, July 1–2, 2017.

Mirembe, Rachel (wedding caterer staff with Daughters of Charity). Interview by author, Nsambya, Kampala, Uganda, July 5, 2017.

Mishra, Pankaj. *Age of Anger: A History of the Present*. New York: Farrar, Straus, and Giroux, 2017.

Morier-Genoud, Eric. *Catholicism and the Making of Politics in Central Mozambique, 1940–1986*. Rochester, NY: University of Rochester Press, 2019.

Mosala, Itumeleng J. *Biblical Hermeneutics and Black Theology in South Africa*. Grand Rapids: Eerdmans, 1989.

Mpiima, John Baptist (retired catechist, Diocese of Kasana-Luweero). Interview with author, Luweero, Uganda, May 28, 2015.

Mugaaga, Robert. "Cardinal Nsubuga: Man of God Amin Never Touched." *The Monitor,* April 26, 2015. http://www.monitor.co.ug/Magazines/PeoplePower/Cardinal-Nsubuga-Man-God-Amin-touched/689844-2697286-11epfkv/index.html.

Mugisa, Anne. "Daughters of Charity founder dies at 74." *The New Vision*, October 9, 2009, 4. https://www.newvision.co.ug/news/1234968/daughters-charity-founder-dies.

Muhima, Edward. "Fellowship of His Suffering: A Theological Interpretation of Christian Suffering under Idi Amin." PhD diss., Northwestern University, 1982.

Mukasa, Stephen, et al. *The Late Emmanuel Cardinal Kiwanuka Nsubuga: 1914-1991*. Kisubi, Uganda: Marianum, 1991.

Mukasa, Willy. "The Day Kabaka Muteesa 'Beat Up' the Catholic Archbishop, *Weekly Topic*, 31 January 1992." In *Bendicto Kagimu Mugumba Kiwanuka: A Martyr of Truth and Justice, Proposal to Open Process for Beatification in Archdiocese of Kampala*, Appendix 29. Kampala: n.p., 2014.

Murungi, Paul. "National Dialogue: Lessons Uganda can Draw from Benin, DR Congo." *The Daily Monitor*, May 12, 2019. https://www.monitor.co.ug/Magazines/PeoplePower/National-dialogue-Lessons-Uganda-Benin-DR-Congo-Tandon-/689844-5110910-cqbtjx/index.html.

Mutibwa, Phares. *The Buganda Factor in Uganda Politics*. Kampala: Fountain, 2008.

Muyingo, John Chrysostom (Uganda State Minister for Higher Education). Interview by author, Kampala, Uganda, May 22, 2019.

Mwebe, Simon (former journalist for *Munno* newspaper). Interview by author, Kampala, Uganda, July 12, 2017.

Nabudere, Dani Wadada. "External and Internal Factors in Uganda's Continuing Crisis." In *Uganda Now: Between Decay and Development*, edited by Holger B. Hansen and Michael Twaddle, 299–312. London: James Currey, 1988.

Nalugo, Annette (former beneficiary of Daughters of Charity). Interview by author, Kiwanga Integrated Skills Training Center, Jinja Road, Uganda, July 8, 2017.

Nalwanga, Allen. "Sister Muyinza: A Mother to Orphans." Pamphlet, Centre for African Christian Studies, Kampala, Uganda, May 2007.

Namazzi, Specioza (former Daughters of Charity beneficiary and staff at Kiwanga Training Center). Interview by author, Kiwanga Integrated Skills Training Center, Jinja Road, July 8, 2017.

Namuddu, Pauline, and Paul G. D'Arbela. "The Congregation of the Little Sisters of St. Francis of Assisi." In *The Catholic Church in Africa: The Uganda Perspective in the Pontificate of Pope Francis*, edited by Antonia Namuli et. al., 110–20. Kisubi, Uganda: Marianum, 2015.

Nanseera, Vincent (priest of Diocese of Masaka and nephew of John Mary Waliggo). Interview with author, Masaka, Uganda, May 7, 2019.

Nassuuna, Gorrette. "Catholic Health Services in Uganda." In *The Catholic Church in Africa: The Uganda Perspective in the Pontificate of Pope Francis*, edited by Antonia Namuli et al., 204–8. Kisubi, Uganda: Marianum, 2015.

Ndarhuka, Dominic (lay catechist, Diocese of Kasana-Luweero). Interview by author, Luwero, Uganda, May 28, 2015.

Newman, John Henry. *Apologia Pro Vita Sua.* Library Newman folder, BKMKP.

Nsubuga, Emmanuel. "Address to Makerere Students Guild at Beginning of 1968 Scholastic Year." February 7, 1968, RDA.

———. "Christmas Message 1966." Pastoral letter, December 1966, RDA.

———. Correspondence to General Tito Okello Lutwa. August 11, 1985, RDA.

———. "Easter Message 1969." Pastoral letter, 1969, RDA.

———. "For God and My Country." Pastoral letter, 1967, RDA.

———. "Message of His Eminence Emmanuel Cardinal Nsubuga Archbishop of Kampala for Commemoration of Victims of Violence on All Souls Day 1980." Pastoral letter, October 30, 1980, RDA.

———. "*Obudde Bw'Amatuuka*" (The Advent Time). Pastoral letter, October 7, 1981, RDA.

———. "*Obudde Obw'ekisiibo*" (Lent Period). Pastoral letter, February 16, 1973, RDA.

———. "*Okukuza Ekyasa Eky'ekkula Lya Batismu*" (Celebrating a Century of the Gift of Baptism). Pastoral letter, February 2, 1980.

———. "Points to be Discussed with the Leaders of the Different Fighting Groups." September 7, 1985, RDA.

———. "Press Conference." January 21, 1986, RDA.

———. "Press Statement of His Eminence Emmanuel Cardinal K. Nsubuga Concerning the Events of Ash Wednesday, 24 February, 1982 at Rubaga Cathedral." March 1, 1982, RDA.

———. "A Statement by H. E. Emmanuel Cardinal K. Nsubuga to the Head of State, Leader of the Government Side, and Leader of the Opposition: My Concern over the Prevailing Situation in Uganda." May 12, 1981, RDA.

———. "Tweyambise Obudde Bw'amatuuka Mu Kwetegekera Ekijaguzo Eky'emyaka Ekikumi" ("Let Us Use the Advent Period to Prepare for the Centennial"). Pastoral letter, November 9, 1977, RDA.

Nsubuga, Frankline Mbamanya (former social worker at Daughters of Charity). Interview by author, Kampala, Uganda, July 14, 2017.

Nyamiti, Charles. *Christ as Our Ancestor: Christology from an African Perspective.* Gweru, Zimbabwe: Mambo, 1984.

Ocen P'akec, Cyprian (priest and former director of Archdiocese of Gulu's Justice and Peace Commission). Interview by author, Padong Parish, Gulu District, July 17, 2017.

Odong, Geoffrey (worked with FORAMO [Forum for Rights Awareness and Human Rights Monitoring Organization]). Interview with author, Gulu, Uganda, November 28, 2018.

O'Grady, Siobhán. "A New Report Estimates that More than 380,000 People have Died in South Sudan's Civil War." *The Washington Post*, September 26, 2018. https://www.washingtonpost.com/world/africa/a-new-report-estimates-more-than-380000-people-have-died-in-south-sudans-civil-war/2018/09/25/e41fcb84-c0e7-11e8-9f4f-a1b7af255aa5_story.html?arc404=true.

Ogwal, Consi (member of Concerned Parents' Association Lira). Interview by author, Lira, Uganda, July 16, 2017.

O'Keefe, John, dir. *Mato Oput.* 2011; Omaha, NE: Creighton University's Backpack Journalism program. https://vimeo.com/33414929/.

Okello, Lawrence. "Catholic Founded Primary and Secondary Schools in Uganda: A Journey of Great Success." In *The Catholic Church in Africa: The Uganda Perspective in the Pontificate of Pope Francis*, edited by Antonia Namuli et al., 134–44. Kisubi, Uganda: Marianum, 2015.

Okot, Yasinto (diocesan program officer, Justice and Peace Commission, Archdiocese of Gulu). Interview by author, Gulu, Uganda, November 28, 2018.

Omona, George, and Rosalba Oywa. "The Plight of Children in Conflict: The Magnitude of the Challenge." Unpublished paper, Uganda-Sudan Religious Leaders' Consultative Meeting, Acholi Religious Leader's Peace Initiative, 2001.

O'Neil, Robert. *Mission to the Upper Nile*. London: St. Joseph's Missionary Society, 1999.

Onen, Prudence Joan (Production Assistant, Radio Pacis). Interview by author, Radio Pacis, Arua, Uganda, October 8, 2018.

Opongo, Elias Omondi. "At the Frontlines of Political Diplomacy: Archbishop Odama's Political Engagement with the LRA Rebels and Government Leadership." In *Catholic Church Leadership in Peacebuilding in Africa*, edited by Elias O. Opongo and David Kaulema, 62–71. Nairobi: Paulines Publications Africa, 2014.

Orobator, Agbonkhianmeghe E., ed. *The Church We Want: African Catholics Look to Vatican III*. Maryknoll, NY: Orbis, 2016.

———. *From Crisis to Kairos: The Mission of the Church in the Time of HIV/AIDS, Refugees, and Poverty*. Nairobi: Paulines Publications Africa, 2005.

———. *Theology Brewed in an African Pot*. Maryknoll, NY: Orbis, 2008.

Otim, Quilinous (founder and director of Ave Maria Vocational Training and Youth Development Center Lira). Interview by author, Lira, Uganda, July 16, 2017.

Otonga, Pelegrine (field reporter, Radio Wa Lira). Interview by author, Lira, Uganda, July 16, 2017.

Oywa, Rosalba Ato. "International Conference on Women and Peacebuilding in Africa (Kampala)." Unpublished paper, May 1–3, 2018.

———. Interview by author, Gulu, Uganda, July 17, 2017.

———. Interview by author, Kampala, Uganda, September 25, 2018.

———. Interview by author, Gulu, Uganda, November 26, 2018.

———. "PANOS—Uganda Briefing." Unpublished paper, Gulu, 1994.

———. "Some of the Challenges of Internally-Displaced Persons (IDPs) Situation in Northern Uganda." Unpublished paper, January 2001.

Oywa, Rosalba Ato, and People's Voice for Peace. "Human Rights Monitoring and Documentation of Torture Incidences in Gulu District, Northern Uganda." Unpublished paper, 2004.

Parsons, Timothy. *The African Rank-and-File: Social Implications of Colonial Military Service in the King's African Rifles, 1902–1964*. Portsmouth, UK: Heinemann, 1999.

Pasolini, Tonino. "Homily for Daniel Comboni Day." Comboni Sisters' Residence, Arua, Uganda, October 10, 2018.

———. Interview by author, Radio Pacis, Arua, Uganda, July 1–2, 2017.

Paul VI. *Populorum Progressio: On the Development of Peoples*. Encyclical Letter, March 26, 1967. http://www.vatican.va/content/paul-vi/en/encyclicals/documents/hf_p-vi_enc_26031967_populorum.html.

p'Bitek, Okot. *Religion of the Central Luo*. Nairobi: Kenya Literature Bureau, 1978.

Perkins, John. "CCDA 2006 Dr. John Perkins Sermon: Thursday Morning Bible Study, Christian Community Development Association (CCDA) Annual Conference." https://www.youtube.com/watch?v=bU_nZKsg-yM.

Pinkman, Kathryn. *A Centenary of Faith: Planting the Seed in Northern Uganda*. Kampala: Comboni Missionaries of the Heart of Jesus, 2010.

Pius XII. *Fidei Donum: On the Present Conditions of the Catholic Missions, Especially in Africa*. Encyclical letter, April 21, 1957. http://w2.vatican.va/content/pius-xii/en/encyclicals/documents/hf_p-xii_enc_21041957_fidei-donum.html.

Pontifical Council of Justice and Peace. *Compendium of the Social Doctrine of the Church*. Washington, DC: Libreria Editrice Vaticana, 2005.

Radio Pacis, "Assessing the Impact of Radio Pacis on Development in the West Nile Region Uganda." Unpublished working paper, 2018.

Ray, Benjamin C. *Myth, Ritual and Kingship in Buganda*. New York: Oxford University Press, 1991.

Rector of Pius XII College (Basutoland). Correspondence to Benedicto Kiwanuka, April 5, 1952. Hon the Chief Justice–Ranch Scheme Folder, BKMKP.

"Refugee Law Project." https://www.refugeelawproject.org.

Reid, Richard. *A History of Modern Uganda*. Cambridge: Cambridge University Press, 2017.

"Remembering Benedicto Kiwanuka." *The Judiciary Insider* 11, September 2018. Kampala, Uganda. http://judiciary.go.ug/files/publications/JudiciaryInsiderIssue11webversion.pdf.

Reticker, Gini, dir. *Pray the Devil Back to Hell*. 2008; New York: Fork Films.

"Rosalba Ato Oywa." https://www.1000peacewomen.org/en/network/1000-peacewomen/search/rosalba-ato-oywa-966-27.html. Also published in *1000 Peacewomen Across the Globe*. Zurich: Kontrast-Verlag, 2005.

Rowe, John A. "Islam under Idi Amin: A Case of Déjà vu?" In *Uganda Now: Between Decay and Development*, edited by Holger B. Hansen and Michael Twaddle, 267–79. Athens: Ohio University Press, 1988.

Rweza, Zachary Anthony (priest of Archdiocese of Kampala and former roommate of John Mary Waliggo). Interview by author, Nsambya, Kampala, May 8, 2019.

Saboni, Jesca O., ed. "Uganda Human Rights Commission and the Uganda Police Force: Human Rights Training Manual." 1st ed. Kampala: n.p., 1999.

Sanneh, Lamin. *Translating the Message: The Missionary Impact on Culture*. 2nd ed. Maryknoll, NY: Orbis, 2009.

Scaperlanda, Maria Ruiz. *Rosemary Nyirumbe: Sewing Hope in Uganda*. Collegeville, MN: Liturgical, 2019.

Scherz, China. *Having People, Having Heart: Charity, Sustainable Development, and Problems of Dependence in Central Uganda*. Chicago: University of Chicago Press, 2014.

Second Vatican Council. *Gaudium et Spes*. Pastoral Constitution on the Church in the Modern World, December 7, 1965. http://www.vatican.va/archive/hist_councils/ii_vatican_council/documents/vat-ii_const_19651207_gaudium-et-spes_en.html.

———. *Lumen Gentium*. Dogmatic Constitution on the Church, November 21, 1964. https://www.vatican.va/archive/hist_councils/ii_vatican_council/documents/vat-ii_const_19641121_lumen-gentium_en.html.

———. *Nostra Aetate*. Declaration on the Relation of the Church to Non-Christian Religions, October 28, 1965. http://www.vatican.va/archive/hist_councils/ii_vatican_council/documents/vat-ii_decl_19651028_nostra-aetate_en.html.

————. *Unitatis Redintegratio*. Decree on Ecumenism, November 21, 1964. http://www.vatican.va/archive/hist_councils/ii_vatican_council/documents/vat-ii_decree_19641121_unitatis-redintegratio_en.html.

Sekaggya, Margaret (former chair of Uganda Human Rights Commission). "Eulogy at Fr. John Mary Waliggo's funeral." Masaka, Uganda: n.p., April 2009.

————. Interview by author, Kampala, Uganda, February 26, 2019.

Sekeba, Drake S. *The Media Bullets in Uganda: A Reference Guide to History of Newspapers, Their Role in Church and Politics of Uganda*. Kampala: Angel, 2016.

Shorter, Aylward. *Cross and Flag in Africa: The "White Fathers" During the Colonial Scramble, 1892–1914*. Maryknoll, NY: Orbis, 2006.

Southern African Catholic Bishops' Conference. "Lumko Institute." http://www.sacbc.org.za/about-us/associate-bodies/lumko-institute/

Ssemogerere, Paul (Bishop of Kasana-Luweero Diocese and former parish priest at Christ the King Kampala). Interview by author, Luweero, Uganda, May 27, 2019.

Ssempereza, Anthony. "Sr. Muyinza abadde nʼomutima ogwa zaabu: Alese ba mulekwa 600" ("Sr. Muyinza had a Golden Heart: Has Left 600 Orphans"). *Bukedde*, October 18, 2009, 1.

Ssenngendo, Charles (former personal secretary to Cardinal Emmanuel Nsubuga). Interview by author, Rubaga, Kampala, Uganda, June 29, 2015.

Ssentle, Jude (headmaster of St. Kizito Sabina School). Interview by author, Rakai, Uganda, February 10, 2019.

Sserwanga, George (retired priest of Diocese of Masaka and professor emeritus, Katigondo Major Seminary). Interview by author, Katigondo, Masaka, Uganda, December 12, 2018.

Ssettuuma, Benedict, Jr. (priest, professor of missiology, and nephew of John Mary Waliggo). Interview with author, Ggaba, Kampala, Uganda, June 26, 2015.

————. Interview by author, Ggaba, Kampala, Uganda, July 6, 2017.

————. *The Thief on the Plane: The Life, Career, Death and Legacy of John Mary Waliggo 18 July 1942–19 April 2008*. Kampala: Angel, 2008.

Ssettuuma, Benedict, Jr., et al. "The Social Teaching of the Uganda Catholic Bishops: 1962–2012." *The Waliggo* 4.2 (2013) 7–50.

Stinton, Diane B. *Jesus of Africa: Voices of Contemporary African Christology*. Maryknoll, NY: Orbis, 2006.

Streicher, Henri. "Appel à la charité des neophytes en faveur des blesses de la guerre, No. 129, Villa Maria, 5 September 1916." In *Instructions Pastorales de Son Excellence Monseigneur Streicher Vicaire Apostolique de L'Uganda à ses Missionnaires Vol. 2 (1910-1932)*, 119. Villa Maria, Uganda: n.p., 1933.

Sundkler, Bengt, and Christopher Steed. *A History of the Church in Africa*. Cambridge: Cambridge University Press, 2001.

Tebesigwa, Tadeo (staff at St. Kizito Sabina School and former beneficiary of Daughters of Charity). Interview by author, Rakai, Uganda, February 10, 2019.

Tegamanyi, Josephine (former beneficiary of Daughters of Charity). Interview by author, Luweero, Uganda, April 27, 2019.

Tinkasiimire, Theresa. "Women, Peacebuilding and Reconciliation in East Africa: A Case of Uganda." In *Peacebuilding in East Africa: Exploring the Role of the Churches*, edited by Paddy Musana, 67–79. Nairobi: Paulines Publications Africa, 2013.

Tombs, David. *Latin American Liberation Theology*. Boston: Brill, 2002.

Tourigny, Yves. *A Century of Trials and Blessings*. Kampala: Uganda Episcopal Conference, 1978.

———. *So Abundant a Harvest: The Catholic Church in Uganda, 1879–1979*. London: Darton, Longman and Todd, 1979.

Tripp, Aili M. *Museveni's Uganda: Paradoxes of Power in a Hybrid Regime*. Boulder, CO: Lynne Reiner, 2010.

———. *Women and Power in Postconflict Africa*. New York: Cambridge University Press, 2015.

Tusingire, Frederick. *The Evangelisation of Uganda: Challenges and Strategies*. Kisubi, Uganda: Marianum, 2003.

Tutu, Desmond. "The Theology of Liberation in Africa." In *African Theology en Route*, edited by Kofi Appiah-Kubi and Sergio Torres, 162–68. Maryknoll, NY: Orbis, 1979.

Twaddle, Michael. "The Emergence of Politico-Religious Groupings in Late Nineteenth-Century Uganda." *Journal of African History* 29.1 (1988) 81–92.

Uganda Episcopal Conference. "I Have Heard the Cry of My People." Joint Pastoral Letter, November 11, 1980, RDA.

———. "In God We Trust." Joint Pastoral Letter, Christmas 1982, RDA.

———. "With a New Heart and a New Spirit." Joint Pastoral Letter, June 29, 1986, RDA.

Uganda Human Rights Commission. "1997 Annual Report." Kampala: n.p., 1998.

———. "Annual Report 1999." Kampala: n.p., 2000.

———. "Annual Report January 2001–September 2002." Kampala: n.p., 2002.

———. "6th Annual Report 2003." Kampala: n.p., 2004.

Ugandan Religious Leaders. "In Search for Peace and Development for Our Nation Uganda: Proposed Background Thoughts for Discussion with Government Leaders and Points to Form a Basis for Discussion between Religious Leaders and the President and Government Officials." 24 September 1981, Dossier 911, Folio 4, RDA.

"Uganda Peace: Women Demand More Role." *The Black Star News*, November 13, 2007. http://www.blackstarnews.com/global-politics/others/uganda-peace-women-demand-more-role.html.

Uganda Women's Network (UWONET) and People's Voice for Peace (PVP). "Report on Situation of Women in Armed Conflict Areas and Peacebuilding in Northern Uganda." Unpublished paper, December 2–4, 1998.

"UJCC Agenda, 9 November 1973." Reel 72, Office of the Archbishop, ACU.

Urban Dictionary. "Street." https://www.urbandictionary.com/define.php?term=Street.

Van Klinken, Adriaan. "Christianity and Same-Sex Relationships in Africa." In *The Routledge Companion to Christianity in Africa*, edited by Elias K. Bongmba, 487–501. New York: Routledge, 2016.

Waliggo, John Mary. "The Catholic Church and the Root-Cause of Political Instability in Uganda." In *Religion and Politics in East Africa: The Period since Independence*, edited by Holger B. Hansen and Michael Twaddle, 106–19. Athens: Ohio University Press, 1995.

———. "The Catholic Church in the Buddu Province of Buganda, 1879–1925." PhD diss., University of Cambridge, 1976. Published posthumously under the same title by Angel Agencies, Kampala, 2011.

———. "The Challenging Vision of the Church in Africa in the 21st Century, *The New People*, c. 1999." In *John Mary Waliggo: Essential Writings 1994–2000*, edited by Benedict Ssettuuma Jr., 1021–26. Kampala: n.p., 2002.

———. "Children's Rights in the New Constitution: Paper to Ministry of Gender and Community Development, 23 April 1996." In *John Mary Waliggo: Essential Writings 1994–2000*, edited by Benedict Ssettuuma Jr., 1125–33. Kampala: n.p., 2002.

———. "Christian Ethics and Leadership in a Democracy of Diversity: Response to Michael Cassidy's Tribute to the Late Bishop Festo Kivengere, Uganda International Conference Center, 21 May 2000." In *John Mary Waliggo: Essential Writings 1994–2000*, edited by Benedict Ssettuuma Jr., 885–91. Kampala: n.p., 2002.

———. "The Church and Politics in Conflict Resolution, 12 March 1999: Paper for National Workshop on Conflict Resolution at Namboole." In *John Mary Waliggo: Essential Writings 1994–2000*, edited by Benedict Ssettuuma Jr., 457–67. Kampala: n.p., 2002.

———. "Church and Politics in the Second Independence of Africa: The Role of Priests and Missionaries, 8 September 1995, Philosophy Center Jinja." In *John Mary Waliggo: Essential Writings 1994–2000*, edited by Benedict Ssettuuma Jr., 467–77. Kampala: n.p., 2002.

———. "The Church and the Revolutionary Process in Uganda, Vienna, May 1989." In *John Mary Waliggo: Essential Writings 1994–2000*, edited by Benedict Ssettuuma Jr., 1026–43. Kampala: n.p., 2002.

———. "Cultural Practices, Customs, and Traditions which Undermine Justice and Human Rights in Family, Church and Society: Workshop on Implementing the African Synod, Nsambya, October 1996." In *John Mary Waliggo: Essential Writings 1994–2000*, edited by Benedict Ssettuuma Jr., 677–81. Kampala: n.p., 2002.

———. "Development of Religious Life in Africa and its Context in the Socio-Political Situation in Africa and the Evangelising Mission of the Church Towards the Year 2000: Paper to Capitulars of Apostles of Jesus, Nairobi (23 Feb. 1996)." In *John Mary Waliggo: Essential Writings 1994–2000*, edited by Benedict Ssettuuma Jr., 251–65. Kampala: n.p., 2002.

———. "Ecumenism in Uganda in the New Millennium: Evaluation and the Way Forward, UJCC Plenary Assembly, 1 June 2000." In *John Mary Waliggo: Essential Writings*, edited by Benedict Ssettuuma Jr., 406–18. Kampala: n.p., 2002.

———. "Education for Resistance, 22 February 2000, National Teachers College, Nkozi, Mitala-Maria Campus." In *John Mary Waliggo: Essential Writings 1994–2000*, edited by Benedict Ssettuuma Jr., 508–17. Kampala: n.p., 2002.

———. "The Evaluation of Catholic Social Teaching in Africa: Statements and Practice (Continental Workshop, Dimisse Sisters, Nairobi, Kenya, 12-15 March 1990)." In *John Mary Waliggo: Essential Writings 1994–2000*, edited by Benedict Ssettuuma Jr., 1156–86. Kampala: n.p., 2002.

———. *A History of African Priests: Katigondo Major Seminary 1911–1986.* Kisubi, Uganda: Marianum, 1988.

———. "How Constitutional is this Referendum? *The New Vision*, February 17, 1999." In *John Mary Waliggo: Essential Writings 1994–2000*, edited by Benedict Ssettuuma Jr., 754–59. Kampala: n.p., 2002.

———. "The Link between Violence, Insecurity, and Poverty in Uganda: Appreciation, Critique and Challenge, Makerere University, 30 January 2001." In *John Mary Waliggo: Essential Writings 1994–2000*, edited by Benedict Ssettuuma Jr., 968–78. Kampala: n.p., 2002.

———. "The Major Challenges to Catholic Missionaries of the Political, Religious, and Cultural Movements in Contemporary Africa, 25 July 1996, sharing with Comboni

Missionaries, Entebbe." In *John Mary Waliggo: Essential Writings 1994–2000*, edited by Benedict Ssettuuma Jr., 279–93. Kampala: n.p., 2002.

———. *The Man of Vision, Archbishop J. Kiwanuka*. Kisubi, Uganda: Marianum, 1992.

———. "The New Constitution and New Approaches in the Protection of Human Rights: Achievements and Challenges, NRM Annual Journal, 26 January 1999." In *John Mary Waliggo: Essential Writings 1994–2000*, edited by Benedict Ssettuuma Jr., 694–702. Kampala: n.p., 2002.

———. "Priests and Politics in Uganda Today: UNDIPA Executive Meeting, 30 January 1996." In *John Mary Waliggo: Essential Writings 1994–2000*, edited by Benedict Ssettuuma Jr., 478–89. Kampala: n.p., 2002.

———. "The Role of Christian Churches in the Democratisation Process in Uganda 1980–1993." In *The Christian Churches and the Democratisation of Africa*, edited by Paul Gifford, 205–24. Leiden: Brill, 1995.

———. "The Role of Culture and Religion in Authentic Development of Africa, Theologie Interkulturell, Johann Wolfgang Goethe-Universitat Frankfurt Am Main, Frankfurt, Germany, Undated." In *John Mary Waliggo: Essential Writings 1994–2000*, edited by Benedict Ssettuuma Jr., 929–51. Kampala: n.p., 2002.

———. "Some Key Lessons from the Uganda Popular Constitution-Making Process (1986–1995), Conference on Nigerian Constitution 2000 at City College, NYC, March 23–24, 2000." In *John Mary Waliggo: Essential Writings 1994–2000*, edited by Benedict Ssettuuma Jr., 703–17. Kampala: n.p., 2002.

———. *Struggle for Equality: Women and Empowerment in Uganda*. Eldoret, Kenya: AMECEA Gaba, 2002.

———. "A Synopsis of the State of Constitutional Struggle in Uganda and the Role of the Uganda Human Rights Commission in Constitution Education: An International Conference on Constitutionalism in Africa, International Conference Center, Kampala, 5-8 Oct. 1999." In *John Mary Waliggo: Essential Writings 1994–2000*, edited by Benedict Ssettuuma Jr., 718–26. Kampala: n.p., 2002.

———. "The Task of Inculturation in the Life and Ministry of African Priests: Meaning, Theory, Principles, and Models, St. Augustine's Institute Nsambya, March 2, 2000." In *John Mary Waliggo: Essential Writings 1994–2000*, edited by Benedict Ssettuuma Jr., 1012–20. Kampala: n.p., 2002.

Waliggo, John Mary, and Denis Mayanja. *Political Education: Vote Maturely*. Tororo, Uganda: Tororo Communications Center, 1980.

Wamala, Emmanuel (retired Cardinal Archbishop of Kampala). Interview by author, Nsambya, Kampala, June 25, 2015.

Ward, Kevin. "Archbishop Janani Luwum: The Dilemmas of Loyalty, Opposition and Witness in Amin's Uganda." In *Christianity and the African Imagination: Essays in Honour of Adrian Hastings*, edited by David Maxwell and Ingrid Lawrie, 199–224. Leiden: Brill, 2013.

———. "The Church of Uganda Amidst Conflict: The Interplay between Church and Politics in Uganda since 1962." In *Religion and Politics in East Africa: The Period since Independence*, edited by Holger B. Hansen and Michael Twaddle, 72–105. London: James Currey, 1995.

Wasswa, Anatoli (Catholic brother, historian, and scholar of local religion). Interview by author, Bunga, Kampala, Uganda, June 30, 2015.

Wasswa Mpagi, Peter (former priest and friend of John Mary Waliggo). Interview by author, Ggaba, Kampala, Uganda, July 21, 2017.

Weber, Max. "Politics as a Vocation, 28 January 1919." http://anthropos-lab.net/wp/wp-content/uploads/2011/12/Weber-Politics-as-a-Vocation.pdf.

"'We're Innocent,' Say Expelled Uganda Priests." *The Daily Nation*, Kampala, Uganda, January 20, 1967.

Whitmore, Todd D. *Imitating Christ in Magwi: An Anthropological Theology.* London: T. & T. Clark, 2019.

Yasinto, Okot (worked with the Archdiocese of Gulu's Justice and Peace Commission at the time of the interview). Interview by author, Gulu, Uganda, November 28, 2018.